ONE STEP AT A TIME

One Step at a Time
The Story of
The Harpenden Group

Copyright © 2011 Martin Hogan

Cover background © 2010 Luke Hogan
Cover design © 2011 Martin Hogan

British Library Cataloguing in Publication Data.
A catalogue record for this book is available from the British Library.

ISBN 0-9549273-1-1

Published by Raise Him Up Christian Publications
444, Buckfield Road,
Leominster,
Herefordshire,
HR6 8SD
England
http://www.rhupublications.com
email:sales@rhupublications.com

First Published 2011

One Step at a Time

The Story of
The Harpenden Group

Martin Hogan

RHU
PUBLICATIONS

Dedication

To Dawson and Norah Price, who set us on the pathway to a deeper relationship with Jesus Christ. Thank you both for shining with the love of the Lord, and for always being there for us, even when you were taken up with a young and demanding family. Thank you also for the years of fellowship together and the fun we have had.

Also to David and Alma Pinkney for giving up their home to a crowd of youngsters and for all your love, generosity and wisdom.

Table of Contents

FOREWORD
By The Reverend Dawson Price BA. OBE.

At the end of Mark's gospel, we are told that, *"The disciples went out and preached everywhere, and the Lord worked with them"*. (Mark 16, 20)

The story in this book is about that sort of partnership between the Lord and a group of Christians, which resulted in dozens of people coming to faith in Jesus, some being healed and others being prepared for fruitful Christian ministries.

What happened was not planned. Nor was it achieved by special human abilities or techniques. The Group simply tried to discern what God was doing, and to fit in with it.

That was why the pattern of a weekly prayer meeting and a weekly Bible discussion meeting, forcefully advocated by Bill Kemp, came to be adopted. We listened to God at the prayer meetings and worked with him at the Bible meetings and also in the other informal contacts with people, which kept on happening week after week.

I have found it fascinating, in this book, to read about the perspective of others on what was happening.

For me there was special enjoyment in praying with so many people, of varying ages and backgrounds, as they received Jesus into their lives. There was also great joy in working with other Christians, who had gifts that I did not have. I enjoyed seeing Bill and Martin getting alongside the young people, mentoring them, and imparting enthusiasm for them. I am no good at music, and it was was good that the Lord brought along Stuart and Sandy, Ruth and others, with fine musical talent, to enrich our meetings.

I look back with praise to the Lord, on all that happened, and I am delighted that Martin and Lorna have been led to tell the story so very well.

My hope is that many Christians will be inspired by it to work with the Lord in bringing thousands of new believers into His Kingdom, and into the blessing that life with Jesus brings.

Dawson Price
28th March 2011

Part 1 The Story
Beginnings

It was 5 am in early June 2009, while I was enjoying an early morning walk with the Lord, that He told me I was to write this book. He said it was to be an accurate account, history and reflection of The Harpenden Group, forty years on.

My first reaction was, "Who would be interested in the goings on of a small group of young Christians establishing their walk with the Lord?" I couldn't understand at first why something so local, that happened so long ago, could be of interest to Christians in the twenty-first century.

As I continued my walk He flooded my mind with thoughts and memories of how we, as young people seeking to serve Jesus, had devoured books about the Welsh Revival at the turn of the twentieth century, and of the excitement we felt, as we read about Billy Bray the Cornish miner, and Smith Wigglesworth in Yorkshire. Then there were the books like The Cross and the Switchblade[1], Run Baby Run[2], Nine O'clock in the

---

1 *The Cross and the Switchblade* was written in 1963 by pastor David Wilkerson with John and Elizabeth Sherrill. It tells the true story of Wilkerson's first five years in New York City, where he ministered to disillusioned youth, encouraging them to turn away from the drugs and gang violence they were involved with. The book became a best seller, with more than 15 million copies distributed in over 30 languages. Publisher: Zondervan; New Edition 2002 ISBN: 978-0310248293.

2 *Run, Baby, Run*; Nicky Cruz; Publisher: Bridge-Logos 1988; ISBN 978-0882706306

Morning[3], and many others, which inspired us to reach out of our comfort zone, and to move with the Lord into areas we never dreamed existed. Then the thought came to me that even the Gospel of Jesus Christ is a local story, which has touched the hearts and lives of countless thousands, down two thousand years and in every country of the world. I realised that the Lord's command to "Take the gospel to all men everywhere," is a command to tell our story, a story that I believe is well worth telling.

As my mind reeled with so many thoughts and memories, the Lord said to me that this is not to be my book; it is His book. He wanted it written because He wants to do a new work with a new generation, who didn't live through those exciting times. He showed me that most young people in the early years of the twenty-first century have never heard of the great Charismatic Movement of the seventies and eighties. He wants them to see how He led us, and has been with us every step of the way. I began to get excited about the project. As I rounded the corner and began to walk up the drive towards the Vicarage, a wave of urgency came over me and I knew that this book had to be written, and written immediately!

A few days later I met with an elderly Christian friend, and we were talking about the new wave of revival that is beginning in our land. Our conversation turned to the seventies and he asked me what had

---

3 *Nine O'clock in the Morning*; Dennis J Bennett; Publisher Bridge Publishing Inc 1994: ISBN 978-0882706290

happened to the Fountain Trust![4] As I thought about this question I realised that the history of the Charismatic Movement, and particularly of The Group, is hugely relevant to the work God is doing at this time. Our conversation had been centred on the wonderful way in which, in every revival, God raises up young people with huge amounts of energy to be in the front line of evangelism. As these young Christians become leaders, they look back, and desire to learn from the past. Today's young leaders look back to the past that we lived through! The Lord also showed me that most of those who were converted, blessed and put on their spiritual walk through The Group, in the sixties and seventies, are still alive today, and are already the main support for the young evangelists and teachers of this century. My prayer is that, through the pages of this book, as I recall those heady days, many will be inspired and encouraged, and that they will look again at their lives and make a recommitment to the Lord Jesus Christ. The revival of the twenty first century will be far greater in its effect and influence than anything that has gone before. However, it will be built on the ongoing experience of the people of God down the ages and through every generation.

In writing this account I have consulted with others involved in The Group. Dawson Price gave me the written records he had collected over more than thirty years. These records contain lists of names, testimonies,

---

4 *The Fountain Trust* was an ecumenical agency formed in the UK in 1964 to promote the Charismatic Renewal. The Trust operated on the principle that it was the purpose of the Holy Spirit to "renew the historic churches". It was founded by Reverend Michael Harper and continued until its voluntary dissolution in 1980. In 1966 the trust set up Renewal Magazine, which for several decades was the leading magazine for Charismatic Christians in the UK.

stories, old newspaper cuttings and newsletters from the time. Bill Kemp, who was such a key person in those early days, has also encouraged me and has been a major source of memories. I have also been in contact with various other people, who remember those days and have kindly given their accounts and testimonies.

However hard one tries, no account will ever be complete, or do full justice to the amazing times we lived through, and the wonderful things we saw and experienced. I was a member of the Group from 1968 to 1984, and therefore have no first hand memories of it, from then until it closed at the turn of the twenty-first century. I have therefore had to rely on the accounts of others. I am very grateful to Virginia Weston and Rosemary Hill for filling me in on those later years.

I want to thank, and pay tribute to Dawson and Norah Price and David and Alma Pinkney, for making their homes available to us for Bible Study and Prayer, and for all their advice and encouragement, which prepared us, and made us ready for a life of ministry and work in the Lord's service. Both couples obediently followed the leading of God, and through their obedience hundreds of people, young and old, found Jesus. I am also indebted to my wife Lorna for her constant encouragement, hours of proof reading and wise advice. Also, thank you to those who have responded to my appeals for material and memories.

I have been greatly encouraged as I have made contact again with so many old friends from those days, and seen how God has used them in ministry and has kept them near. The Group, and all that happened in it, was not a result of any human planning, but was a wonderful work of the Holy Spirit of God, making Jesus known. All credit and glory belongs to God.

To those of you who get as far as finishing this book, I pray that you will discover the same Jesus, who has been such a blessing to us and so many people down the ages. I pray that you too will dare to step out in faith, walk with Him step by step, and find, as we have, a loving, trustworthy, and wonderful Friend and Saviour who guides us one step at a time.

Reverend Martin Hogan
Leominster
February 2011

Chapter 1
The First Step

In the Autumn of 1965 the U.K. Atomic Energy Authority transferred Dawson Price from Harwell, near Oxford, to their London Headquarters, and so he, his wife Norah and their three children, had to move nearer to London. They wanted to settle north of London, as all their relatives lived in the north of England. Harpenden, just half an hour by train into London, was an ideal choice.

Dawson was then 34. He had been a Lay Reader[5] in the Church of England since 1962. He had been involved in an exciting daughter church project in Abingdon, near Oxford, where they had seen the congregation grow, over a period of only three years, from about twenty, meeting once a month, to weekly congregations of around sixty at the 8 am Communion, three hundred at the Family Service, and sixty again at the Evening Service! He preached regularly at the Family and Evening Services. The main emphasis of the church was evangelical. He and others, including the curate, had received the baptism in the Holy Spirit[6], through a prayer meeting out

---

5 *A Lay Reader* is a layperson authorised by a bishop of the Anglican Church to read some parts of a service of worship. They are members of the congregation called to preach or lead services, but not called to full-time ministry.

6 *The Baptism of the Holy Spirit*, sometimes known as the Pentecostal experience, is the experience of Spirit baptism that initiates the believer in the use of the spiritual gifts. See the Gospel of John Chapter 20 verse 22, also Acts 2. Baptism in the Holy Spirit should not be confused with conversion or believer's baptism.

in the country, led by a remarkable woman called Joan Steele. Through this, there was a small but growing charismatic[7] influence in their church.

Harpenden, however, was an unknown quantity and they wondered whether the Lord wanted them to stay in the Church of England. None of the local Anglican churches at the time, seemed to have any interest in evangelism, or had yet been touched by the Charismatic Renewal. They tried the Free Evangelical Church, where there was a keen interest in evangelism, but hostility towards charismatic things.

Eventually he arranged to meet the Rector[8] of St. Nicholas' Parish, the Reverend Peter Graham. Dawson gave his testimony and said that, if he would be an embarrassment to him in the parish, he would try to link up with a parish outside Harpenden. But Peter was warmly welcoming. He confided that he too had been baptised in the Spirit, when Reverend Dennis Bennett from the United States had visited the area. He had kept quiet about it, because he did not think many of his people would understand what had happened. Before Dawson left, the Rector asked if he would be willing to take responsibility for people referred to the parish from

---

7 **Charismatic** comes from the New Testament Greek word *charisma*, meaning 'gift', or 'favoured by God'. It became associated with a renewal movement at the turn of the 20th century, which encouraged the '*Baptism of the Holy Spirit*' and a wider use of the *gifts* of the Holy Spirit.

8 **Rector.** In the Anglican Churches, a rector is one type of parish priest. Historically, parish priests in the Church of England were divided into rectors, vicars, and perpetual curates. Roughly speaking, the distinction was that the rector directly received both the greater and lesser tithes of his parish, and a vicar received only the lesser tithes (the greater tithes going to the lay holder, or impropriator, of the living); a perpetual curate with a small cure and often aged or infirm received neither greater nor lesser tithes, and received only a small salary (paid sometimes by the diocese).

the recent Billy Graham Crusade[9], and perhaps arrange a Bible Study meeting for them.

Like Peter, Dawson was cautious about how to handle the charismatic dimension. The Lord's guidance seemed to be, that they should not mention the subject, unless they were specifically asked about it.

The first group of people met in their home, 8 Springfield Crescent, in the late summer of 1966. Out of those invited, only a few came. When they were invited to ask questions, one young man said: "What I want to know about, is the baptism in the Holy Spirit". His name was Bill Kemp. He had come with his girlfriend, Jacquie Webb. The Rector and Dawson both shared their experience of the Holy Spirit, as did Norah. From then on they felt a God-given freedom to be quite open on the subject, at all meetings of The Group.

Over the next year they met weekly for Bible study. Others joined them, including Angela Keith and her friend Lynn. Bill was keen to have a meeting for prayer as well as the one for Bible study, and so the pattern of two meetings a week, one on Tuesday and the other on Thursday evenings, was established.

In November 1966, they had a visit from the Reverend Leonard Moore of Bedford (C. of E.) He received the Baptism of the Spirit that night and took his experience back to Bedford. In April 1967 we saw our first conversion (Lynn). That same month, Dawson and Norah's family was enlarged to five, by the arrival of twin boys!

---

9 *Billy Graham* is probably the greatest American evangelist ever! He visited the UK in 1954 then again in 1966 and 67 and again in 1984 for Mission England. He is a prolific author and a great man of God.

Then, in the summer of 1967, the Holy Spirit took over in quite a dramatic way. Although the meetings were not advertised, people began phoning up, knocking on the door, or just turning up for meetings. Those who came brought others. Over the next few months numbers at the Bible studies rose to over fifty, with twenty or more at the prayer meetings! That autumn several were baptised in the Holy Spirit, including Big Stewart (Armour), when the Reverend Moore visited us again.

One couple who knocked on the door was David and Alma Pinkney, who had been referred to Dawson by The Fountain Trust, of which Dawson and Norah were keen supporters. Fortunately David and Alma had a much bigger house in Lyndhurst Drive, and became hosts to the weekly Bible studies. The prayer meetings stayed at Springfield Crescent.

In late 1967 we had smaller numbers, and fewer professions of conversion. Almost everyone who has professed conversion during this later period, is still showing evidence of continuing in their faith, whereas we must recognise that some of those, who professed conversion during the rush period from late 1967 to early 1968, have fallen away.

One of the healthy features of that period was the development of Christian initiative and leadership. Several people started to lead the meetings and even began to preach. Many were willing to lead, pray or testify at meetings or services, about how they came to believe in Jesus, and about their Christian experiences since conversion. Most were willing to talk to friends, people they met, and patients at the hospital service, about Jesus.

It was wonderful to see how the enthusiasm of a few, could encourage such a large number of people, and how their confidence and trust in the Lord grew. The most exciting meetings were those where expectation that the Holy Spirit was in control was high. There were accusations that we swung from chandeliers and chewed off door knobs! However, in reality, there was never any hype or undue emotionalism.

We did have, for a time, a middle aged lady who used to breathe very heavily, a practice we called "Huffing and puffing". It was not of the Lord, and many of us were very concerned about it. We talked with Dawson, who suggested that, if it wasn't of the Lord, He would show the lady concerned that it was wrong. At the beginning of the next prayer meeting, she asked our forgiveness for her huffing and puffing, which the Lord had revealed to her was wrong! None of us had mentioned it to her; it was the Lord's business and He dealt with it.

It was wonderful, how well the simple pattern of the Bible study meetings was suited to personal evangelism. In the next chapter I shall describe the meetings and how they worked.

Chapter 2
A Formula that Worked

The Group's approach to Christianity was a simple one. Yet, in spite of its simplicity, it was amazingly and powerfully used by God. We often likened what we did to a three legged stool. Three legs are more stable than four, and they will always stand firm without being shaken, but for a really stable Christian life the three legs need to be about the same length! The first leg is well grounded Bible study. It is very important for spiritual growth. Our studies were always good and solid, like a nourishing meal, founded on the firm acceptance that the Word of God is true and stands forever. Prayer is the second leg. It is vital for building up our relationship with Jesus. It is our conversation with him. We always encouraged prayer to be a personal, honest dialogue with God. Other people's written prayers have their place in the more formal settings of Church services, but have only a small place in the relationship building that is communion with Jesus. Regular fellowship with one another is the third leg. In The Group we found loving acceptance and a safe environment to test what we learned and practise our faith, knowing that if we made mistakes we would not be condemned or thrown out. When we exercised the gifts of the Holy Spirit, we knew that we would not be laughed at or made to feel silly.

The Bible Studies

Everything started with the Bible Study on a Thursday evening. It didn't take us very long to realise the need to place our study into its proper setting, that of worship. Singing became an important part of our gatherings, and we progressed from singing a few well known hymns, to gathering a wealth of hymns, choruses and worship songs from many different traditions. Everything we sang had to be transposed and adapted for guitar accompaniment. At that time there were not many song and chorus books available, which had chords suitable for guitars. Fortunately we had a few good musicians and singers, and some were able to do the necessary tweaking, so we were always able to make a joyful noise to the Lord.

Although the point was never laboured heavily, it was always taken for granted and assumed, that the Bible is the living Word of God, inspired by Him, and therefore has something very special and important to say to us today. It was also accepted that everyone, from the youngest to the oldest in the Lord, has something to contribute, and that the Lord can give his insights to us all. Of course the leader prayerfully prepared the Bible study beforehand, waiting on the Lord for His leading. But we always sought to be prepared for the unexpected, the special need or personal problem, which would arise and deflect the course of the study or prayer into a particular area. We soon learned that the Holy Spirit's way is the best, and those meetings, where we were deflected, were most often the most fruitful. So, although every week had a leader, the discussion that followed was always an unknown quantity, and often included areas of discussion never envisaged. Very often the passage covered in an evening was only a verse or two. This was especially true when we were studying the Gospel of St. John. At other times we might be able to cover many verses and even whole chapters. The secret was to be totally open to where the Lord wanted to lead us, even if it seemed at the time to be off the point.

Dawson was especially sensitive in his leadership, and had the gift of seeing in every comment, something useful, even when the rest of us couldn't see it. No-one was ever put down, or made to feel their contribution was worthless. All were encouraged and built up, and so gained in confidence.

We all used different versions or translations of the Bible, from the King James Authorised Version, to J.B. Phillips. Many of us used the Revised Standard Version or the New English Bible. This all gave the study richness and insight. I remember the sense of excitement and anticipation when the New International Version first came out. We never tried to standardise, for often a passage would become much more real in one version, than in all the others. We really had no time for all the heady theological arguments, which favoured one version over another. God spoke to us all, whatever version we were using.

There was an amazing hunger to read God's Word and to understand it. Often the study would go on after the meeting had finished and into the refreshment time. Amazingly, there were very few heated arguments, as the Holy Spirit opened up and enlarged our minds, to include the understanding and interpretation of others. We found that sharing our understanding, and listening to others, helped to keep us on the straight and narrow path. It was as though sharing openly had its own checks and balances built in.

Personal study was encouraged. Bible reading plans and notes were freely available, including the newly published Every Day With Jesus, compiled by Selwyn Hughes[10].

At the end of every study, we had a time of prayer. Prayer in The Group was rarely, if ever, one person praying. It was open to all to pray aloud, and many did. They were always very rich times. We usually drew it all to a close by joining hands in a circle and saying The Grace together. Tea, coffee and hot chocolate were then prepared.

The Prayer Meetings

The prayer meetings were very special, usually an hour and a half of solid prayer. Yet often the time passed so quickly, we thought it was only a few minutes long! Some people sat on chairs, and some on cushions on the floor. Some prayed aloud, while others were silent. The key was that, although we highlighted prayer needs at the beginning of the meeting, and there were usually a few, we tried to be led by the Holy Spirit. Silences and waiting on the Lord played an important part in our meetings, and there was always complete freedom to use

---

10 *Selwyn Hughes* (27 April 1928 - 9 January 2006) was a Welsh Christian minister best known for writing the daily devotional Every Day with Jesus. He founded the Christian ministry Crusade for World Revival (CWR) and wrote over fifty Christian books. George Carey, the former Archbishop of Canterbury, described Hughes as a "giant in the faith".

the gifts of the Holy Spirit. It was here at these meetings, that we saw the gifts of the Holy Spirit in action. Sometimes we were privileged to see many of the gifts manifest in one evening. Prophecy, words of knowledge, tongues and interpretation of tongues, healing and miracles were all expected and often experienced. At other times it might be only the gift of tongues. On a few occasions, not very often, we felt the need to informally break bread together.

In The Group the individual was more important than the meeting, so planning and a liturgical structure was kept to a minimum. Ritual and repetition played no part in our meetings; it was as though we had no need of them. Total participation from all who attended was encouraged, though never spoken of, and no-one felt pressured. If someone had something to contribute or to pray for, it was always given the necessary space. We relied on the Holy Spirit to cover our mistakes, and to enlighten our hearts and our minds. It was months before I prayed aloud in a meeting and I well remember my heart pounding in my chest, so that I thought everyone in the room could hear it. It was a faltering prayer, but it was from the heart. At that moment I felt I knew the cost every new Christian pays when first praying aloud, and I have, throughout my ministry, loved to hear, as God must love it, that precious prayer of love.

As I have said, we had little space for formal prayers, except the Lord's Prayer and the prayer of The Grace. I remember at one prayer meeting, becoming aware that the whole meeting took the shape of The Lord's Prayer. It wasn't by human design, but the pattern was clear and each section was echoed by a phrase from His prayer. It was beautiful, but couldn't have been engineered.

The exercise of the gifts of the Spirit was a joy to behold. Every week the Lord astounded us with his infinite variety. The most commonly used gift was undoubtedly the gift of tongues, which most of us received and practised. But even that was never the same. Most often it was a way of communicating directly with the Lord, and we would find ourselves praying quietly together in tongues. Sometimes out of that quiet prayer a tongue would be raised higher than the others and take on a new, more commanding feel. When this happened an interpretation usually followed. The interpretation might take the form of a word, for a particular person or into a specific situation. Sometimes it was a prophetic word for the whole assembly. For a time these special words were written down. After all, if the Lord takes the trouble to speak to us, we should take what He says seriously. It is all too easy to hear and be excited by what He says, and then go out and forget what He said.

On one occasion I began to speak out loud in tongues. I spoke for about two or three minutes, which is quite a long time. Suddenly I stopped, as though in the middle of a sentence. At once someone else took up where I left off, and spoke again for two or three minutes. Once again he stopped mid-sentence and a third person took up the flow. After about two minutes the word came to an end, and instantly I had the beginning of the interpretation, which I shared. But, as in the original word, I stopped mid-sentence, and the second and then the third person took up the flow! The word was a prophecy which was very relevant to us at the time and proved a great help and encouragement. Unlike most tongues and prophetic interpretations, the tongue and the style of interpretation were the same for all three of us, which helped us to accept that the word was from the Lord.

Prophecy and words of knowledge often came in the form of visions or pictures, and were sometimes given to two or three people simultaneously. It was often the case that someone who professed to think in words would see visions, while those of us who think in pictures would speak out words. I love the way God uses our weaknesses!

Fellowship

Dawson was always very keen, and rightly so, not to let The Group become another church denomination or sect, meeting on a Sunday. He always encouraged people to either join a church, or return to their own church, and he always respected their choice. However, in every way, The Group functioned as an organic Church, a fellowship of believers. For many it was their only experience of a real, loving fellowship, where all people were valued. Prayer was real, and the Bible was grounded where the people were. Prayers from the heart often poured out amidst floods of tears. If the Spirit was leading, these prayers were followed by the gentle, loving ministry of the church gathered. A lot of people get hurt by church politics and rivalries, and we did our best to heal those hurts and equip people to ride over them and still stand. Unfortunately, both then and now, churches are very unaccepting of things that fall outside their particular practice or experience. Many of us experienced open hostility to the things of the Spirit, from the very people who should have encouraged and blessed us, our churches!

As people came to the meetings, our prime aim was always to help them establish their own personal relationship with the Lord Jesus, or to deepen an existing relationship. We had learned that you can't force people to believe, or threaten them into a relationship. It had to come from them, and be quickened by the Holy Spirit. Our task was to provide a loving environment, which could make that possible.

We were aware that some problems were rooted in the lack of sound teaching from the denominations people were in. This we sought lovingly to address and rectify, without belittling their church or fellowship. We had members of every mainstream church, and some from churches we had never heard of before. We even had some visitors from the Church of Jesus Christ of the Latter Day Saints[11], with whom we had great fellowship, and visitors from the Jewish faith, and even Jehovah's Witnesses. The unspoken rule was never to denounce any denomination, but to point to Jesus, God's Word, and the truth.

---

11 *The Church of Jesus Christ of Latter-day Saints* (abbreviated as the LDS Church, and colloquially referred to as the Mormon Church) is a restorationist Christian religion and the largest denomination originating from the Latter Day Saint movement founded by Joseph Smith, Jr. in Upstate New York in 1830. The church is headquartered in Salt Lake City, Utah, and has established congregations (called wards or branches) internationally. There are currently over 13 million members of the LDS Church worldwide.

People with Problems

We were soon aware that we live amongst a hurting people, and that many have severe problems. We never sought to probe too deeply into the past, for we knew that if people allowed Jesus to come into their hearts, He would deal with their problems, working from the inside, with His unique understanding of their particular needs. We could only assure them that Jesus offers them perfect forgiveness, a clean start and a new life. When people reached a point when they wanted to talk about the past, we saw that it was our role to listen, to pray, to support and to encourage. Sometimes we were asked directly to give guidance, and in a sense tell them what they should do. Our answer was always to look at God's Word and see what the Bible has to say. If it wasn't clear from the Bible we would pray with them for guidance. Very often the Lord would give us a prophetic word or a word of knowledge. In every case it was a matter of saying what we felt the Lord was saying, but leaving the decision to the individual.

On one occasion, when it was very obvious what was right, but the temptation to do the wrong thing was very strong, we had to say, "The choice is yours, but whatever you decide, we are here for you." On that occasion the person concerned accepted our offer of a bed for the weekend, until the subject of the temptation had moved on. In most cases, people know what is the right thing to do, because God has set in all our hearts a sense of right and wrong. The problem is that Satan, the master of deceit, makes the alternative appear very attractive and harmless.

Fred and Carol, (*not their real names*) were a middle age couple who started attending the Bible Study. They were not married to each other, but living together. Carol had been abandoned by her husband for their young au pair. However she remained married to him. Fred was also married, but had, due partly to his life as an army officer, grown apart from his wife. She had refused him a divorce as she was a Catholic. Both Fred and Carol made a commitment to Jesus, but still remained living together. Some of The Group were very concerned about this situation, especially as the teaching of the Bible is to shun adultery and sex before marriage. They approached Dawson and myself and asked us to challenge Fred and Carol. Both Dawson and I were concerned that we might do more harm than good, so we committed it to prayer. After about a week of praying, the Lord told us to invite Fred and Carol around for a chat. This we did, and we met at Springfield Crescent. Dawson was amazing! Never once did he condemn or accuse, yet somehow, guided by the Holy Spirit, he moved the conversation around to matters of Christian morality, and backed by scripture, told them that their adultery was not God's ideal plan for them. As he spoke, Fred began to weep. We moved into prayer with them, and he confessed his sin and asked for forgiveness. After the prayer time he told us that he had had no idea at all that he was doing wrong; all his mates did it all the time. He resolved, in our presence, to put things right. No one saw him for some months after that, and we wondered if we had overstepped the mark. Then he re-appeared and told us he had been trying to put things right with his wife. She had refused. She had someone else and, in spite of her Catholic beliefs, they started divorce proceedings. At the same time, Carol's husband had a massive heart attack and died. He was only in his late forties. When the divorce became absolute Fred and Carol were married, and after a time they moved away.

We met with a wide variety of problems in people's lives. They were perhaps a reflection of the times in which we live. They included:

- Drugs, notably heroin, LSD[12] and cannabis. Currently some people maintain that cannabis is harmless. If they could see the effects of it in the lives of real people, they would not be able to maintain such views.

- Abortion, or the pain of having to give up a child for adoption.

- The consequences of unsatisfactory relationships or promiscuous lifestyles.

- Pain stemming from the death of loved ones, including suicide.

- The effects of homosexual experiences. One man was devastated when his wife left him for a lesbian relationship. Another earned his living by acting as a homosexual prostitute.

---

12 LSD or Lysergic Acid Diethylamide is a hallucinogenic drug (which means you're likely to experience a distorted view of objects and reality, including in the form of hallucinations). It originally derived from ergot, a fungus found growing wild on rye and other grasses. LSD is commonly called 'acid'.

- Involvement with the occult. This could range from the 'innocent' use of Ouija boards, to witchcraft. Whenever we ministered to people from this background we considered it wise to have at least two others present.

- Criminal activities, including drug pushing.

- Self harm, and anorexia.

Somehow we were given special grace to care for those who came with such problems. Sadly some were not prepared to allow Jesus to meet their needs, and we watched helplessly as they returned to destructive lifestyles. However, if Jesus was allowed into a person's life, remarkable healing, peace and transformation always followed.

Whenever there was a need to minister to drug addicts or other serious problems, Dawson would invite other members of The Group to join him. This served two purposes. Firstly he was not alone in ministry. Others could bring the Lord's word or prophecy into the situation, and be praying, thus allowing the Lord's words to be put into action. *"Again, truly I tell you that if two of you on earth agree about anything they ask for, it will be done for them by my Father in heaven."* Matthew 18:19. Secondly, it was a wonderful training ground for those of us less experienced in dealing with these issues. I'm sure I learned more through being with Dawson, than in my time at theological college and subsequently in ministry!

Dawson's gentle ministry was an inspiration to us all. We often heard him give prophetic words, or words of wisdom, that spoke exactly into the situation, like 'Just take one step at a time.' The following poem, submitted by Carolyn Armour sums up this teaching beautifully. I have included Carolyn's comments:

Dear Martin, I have had this translation and poem on a card for years.... I always thought it summed up the message of The Group. We prayed about many things, but always the over-riding feeling that I came away with, was one of trust, that in everything, we can trust that God is leading us on, and He knows where we are going. He will be there at every turn. It's true! Carolyn Armour.

As Thou Goest, Step By Step

*"As Thou Goest, Step By Step,
I Will Open Up The Way Before Thee."*

Proverbs 4: 12. Hebrew trans.

Child of My love, fear not the unknown morrow,
Dread not the new demand life makes of thee;
Thy ignorance doth hold no cause for sorrow
Since what thou knowest not is known to Me.

Thou canst not see today the hidden meaning
Of My command, but thou the light shalt gain;
Walk on in faith, upon My promise leaning,
And as thou goest all shall be made plain.

One step thou seeest — then go forward boldly,
One step is far enough for faith to see;
Take that, and thy next duty shall be told thee,
For step by step thy Lord is leading thee.

Stand not in fear thy adversaries counting,
Dare every peril, save to disobey;
Thou shalt march on, all obstacles surmounting,
For I, the Strong, will open up the way.

Wherefore go gladly to the task assigned thee,
Having My promise, needing nothing more
Than just to know, where'er the future find thee,
In all thy journeying I go before.

— Selected.

I remember on one occasion, Dawson was approached by a couple who, with another couple, had both been involved in taking drugs, including LSD. They had got themselves into a terrible state, and wanted to be free of it. The woman had previously made a Christian commitment. It was soon apparent that they were possessed by some sort of evil spirits. Dawson called three of us to join him as he counselled and prayed with them. It was quite a long battle, and we were with them until late into the night. Eventually, after lots of prayer, quite a few visions, words of prophecy and knowledge, all four were wonderfully set free, and they all made commitments to the Lord Jesus. One of them described her experience of LSD like having a protective barrier in her mind unlocked, which left her open to all kinds of evil influences. Although she remained true to her commitment to Christ, she still suffered from a bi-polar personality disorder, which had to be controlled by drugs.

Through this and many other instances, we also became aware of the attacks of Satan. If the Lord was about to do something big, or had just done something wonderful, Satan was there trying to disturb our peace and destroy our joy. Often four or five of us would say at the beginning of a meeting, what an awful week or few days we had had, or how minor disasters had happened, like appliances breaking down. When these incidences came in groups, or to three or four people, we always knew that the Lord was at work, and we would turn the Devil's efforts to disrupt us into times of praise. Invariably we were lifted into the heavenly places and saw God at work.

In the mid seventies, a group in St Albans organised monthly meetings called St. Albans Praise, culminating in a service near Pentecost in St. Albans Abbey, called Pentecost Praise. I was asked to speak at one of their monthly meetings, and decided to spend the whole of that Saturday in prayer and fasting. Lorna took our three children, Robin, Maria and Joseph, out for a walk to help keep the house quiet for me. Within half an hour of leaving, Maria came running back to say that Robin had trodden on some glass and would need to be taken to hospital. As I was the only one in the house that could drive, I had to take him to Luton and Dunstable Hospital Casualty Dept, where I spent the entire afternoon waiting around. I arrived home just in time to change and go off to St. Albans Praise! It was a wonderful evening and the Lord blessed it, in spite of me being exhausted and frustrated by the day's events.

Healings were both expected and common in The Group. That's not to say everyone who needed healing was healed. Far from it. However we saw many miracles, some instantaneous, and some over a longer period of time.

One warm, late summer evening we were at a prayer meeting in Dawson's house with all the windows open. The local farmer had been harvesting his crop in the field behind the estate. The air was filled with the smell of newly cut wheat. During the evening one young lady was showing real signs of distress, as her eyes puffed up and her nose began to stream with hay fever. She tried to hide her discomfort, but the Lord revealed it to me, and I knew I had to go and pray for her. After praying with her, the Spirit urged me to just stay there with my hand gently on her shoulder. This I did. Meanwhile the prayer meeting moved on to pray for other things. After about 15 minutes I became aware that her symptoms had reduced to nearly nothing, and after another few minutes they were completely gone. After the meeting she told us that she had always suffered from hay fever, especially at harvest time, and had learnt to live with it. She had dosed herself with antihistamine that day, but to no effect. However, after this prayer, she had no further symptoms during the years I knew her.

A school friend of mine, Roger Keech, joined The Group in the early eighties. We had lost touch for a few years as we had both gone our separate ways. He was, at the time, working at the Cathedral at St Albans as a verger[13].

---

13 *A verger* (or virger, so called after the staff of the office, Latin virga = twig, rod) is a person, usually a layman, who assists in the ordering of religious services, particularly in Anglican churches.

He was greatly blessed by his time in fellowship with us and went on to do evangelism in South Africa. He is now retired and living in Dundee. In August 2009 he reminded me of the following incident. These are his words, (italics mine):

I clearly remember a few of us turned up one evening at your home. *It wasn't a regular meeting,* and you had told us nothing beforehand of what we were going to be praying about, except that you had asked God that only those who were prepared to do true spiritual battle would turn up.

I remember Dawson being there, along with Stewart, myself and you. We learned from you that Lorna's young cousin had been taken in by a cult, The Moonies[14], and that on that very evening another cousin and Lorna's brother, were going to try and get her out, although the cult was known for not letting people go!

We prayed for at least one hour, and at the end of the time everybody felt the lifting of a great burden, all at the same time. This was not because time had run out and we had to go back home, but because we all felt a tremendous sense of peace, that the battle had been won.

Several days after this, when we met again as a group you told us that they had got her out, and had taken her back home. The journey home was at the exact time we felt the lifting of a heavy burden in The Group. I am not sure what happened after that, but events later confirmed that a decisive spiritual battle had been won. *R.K.*

---

14 Moonie (plural Moonies) is sometimes used to refer to members of the Unification Church. This is derived from the name of the church's founder Sun Myung Moon.

Like all soldiers, young Christians like to be where the action is. In the late 60's and all through the 70's there was plenty of action outside of the weekly meetings, some of which I describe in the next chapter.

Chapter 3
Outreach and Revivals

As young Christians become switched on, the Lord puts in their hearts a desire to hear His Word expounded, to be involved in worship and to see His saving power at work in the lives of others. Members of The Group were no exception. We spent many happy hours singing, praying and talking, squashed in the back of Bill Kemp's minibus, along with musical instruments and Bibles, as we travelled to this meeting, or to that chapel. One of our favourite venues was Welwyn Garden City Apostolic Free Church (The Appy Church) where we were always made very welcome. One year they held a mission to the town and we all took part in house-to-house visiting, prayer meetings, and the evening outreach meetings. We also followed some of the great speakers of the day, Peter Scothern[15], David du Plessis[16] and many others.

On one occasion we went to a mission meeting in Welwyn. It was in the dead of winter. When we came out at about 10:30 pm the ground was thickly covered in snow and the roads were like a skating rink. One of our number, a young lady who lived in North London, needed to be taken home, and we all squashed into Bill's minibus. It was a really difficult journey. Conditions were

---

15 http://www.peterscothernministries.com

16 *David Johannes du Plessis* (February 7, 1905 - January 31, 1987) was a South African-born Pentecostal minister, and is considered one of the main founders of the charismatic movement, in which the Pentecostal experience spread to non-Pentecostal churches worldwide.

appalling, and we were getting nowhere fast. Someone suggested we should pray and, almost as though we had snow chains on, we began to make progress. We got her home and managed to drop everyone else safely home. Bill dropped me off last, and I walked through the door at 2am, to find my mother had been woken up by the Lord to pray for our safety! She had got up and remained in prayer until I arrived home. She made me a drink of hot chocolate, and we sat by the kitchen boiler, where she insisted on hearing all about the meeting. Never once did she let on how anxious she had been for us all. God bless all praying mums!

Dawson often had preaching engagements at various churches and chapels around the area. We would take a minibus load of young people, both to swell the congregation, and to pray for him as he preached. He usually asked one of us to give a testimony at some point.

In 1969 The Group was greatly encouraged by the ministry of the American evangelist and teacher, Jean Darnall[17]. We invited her to come to Harpenden Public Hall to conduct a meeting. The turnout was amazing and the evening uplifting. During her time of ministry Jean referred to a vision she had received three times and we were all encouraged and blessed by it. This is one account of what she saw.

Suddenly a vision appeared within my mind. It had come twice before. I saw the British Isles glistening like a clump of jade in the grey seas surrounding them. Looking down I saw

---

17 **Dr Jean Darnall** ministered in Britain for over 25 years and was one of the leading figures in the Charismatic Renewal. In 1967, she saw a vision of a coming revival in the UK, and much of her vision has already become reality. Jean is the author of the bestselling Heaven Here I Come and is on the pastoral staff at The Church on the Way, a large Pentecostal church in California led by Dr Jack Hayford.

Scotland, England, Wales, and to the north-west, Ireland. The treetops upon the hills and the clustered clouds hid the people. Suddenly small flickering fires appeared. They were scattered over the isles. I came closer to the land. The light was firelight. These were fires burning, from the top of Scotland to Land's End on the tip of Cornwall. Lightning streaked downwards from the sky above me. I saw it touch down with flashing swiftness, exploding each of the fires into streams of light. Like lava they burned their fiery path downward from the top of Scotland to Land's End. The waters did not stop this, but the fires spread across the seas to Ireland and to Europe.

"Lord, this is the third time you've shown me this vision during prayer. Could you give me the meaning of it?" I asked, deeply moved by the Holy Spirit. He revealed to me that the small fires were groups of earnest, hungry people who were being drawn together by the Holy Spirit to study their Bibles and to pray for a visitation of the Holy Spirit. The words, 'pockets of power' were impressed upon my mind. "I'm empowering them by my Holy Spirit and I'm teaching them by my Spirit about my gifts. They are being led by my Spirit to repentance, reconciliation and a deeper relationship with the body of Christ. These people are meeting in homes and churches. I'm not leading them out of their relationships in the home and in the church, but into a deeper involvement in both. They are to bring renewal, new life, in preparation for what is to come." "What is to come, Lord?", I asked, wondering why he should show this to me.

"I will penetrate the darkness with a visitation of my power. With lightening swiftness I will release the power of my Spirit through a renewed people who have learned to be led of the Spirit. They will explode with a swiftness that will touch every part of the society of Britain. I am strategically placing them to touch farms, villages, towns and cities. No one will be without a witness, whether they be children in schools, farmers in the fields, workers in the factories and docks, students in the universities and colleges, the media, the press, the arts or government. All will be profoundly moved and those who are changed by my power will alter the destiny of the nation." ·

"And the streams of fire into Europe, Lord?" My mind seemed to see an army of all types of people moving into the continent with a compassionate ministry. This ministry was not mass meetings, led by powerful personalities, preaching to spectators, but participating, caring communities, involved with one another at grass roots level, sharing the love of God everywhere.

The Hospital Service

Some time in the late 60's, Dawson was asked by the Rector of Harpenden, to take a once-a-month service in the day room of the Red House, our local hospital, on Sunday mornings. Most of the patients were geriatric, but there were also a few younger people recovering from minor operations, and some young mums from the maternity wing. Occasionally we had old folk who were staying for a short while, whilst their carers had a rest or holiday.

We soon developed a style and order for these lovely times of worship. We would sing a few hymns, accompanied either on their piano, or with our guitars. We would have a reading from the Bible, a testimony and a short address, followed by prayers, and usually an offer to pray individually with the patients.

Dawson was never possessive about the leadership of the services; indeed he encouraged all of us to take a lead. Sometimes he took no apparent part at all, but was always there in the background. It was a real time of spiritual growth for us. I often think that the young people who took part got more out of those times than the patients, but we were always very well received and welcomed.

On one occasion, Angela, a fifteen year old, who had just given her heart to Jesus, gave her testimony, a simple account of how someone had led her to faith and what a difference it had made to her. At the end of the service Dawson asked if anyone had anything to add or ask, and from the corner an old gentleman, Bill Seymore, who we all thought was asleep, piped up and asked Angela a simple question: *"Angela you say you asked Jesus into your heart, and he came. How do you know He was there?"* We all prayed like mad for her, but she simply replied, *"Oh I know He came in because I talked with Him this morning."* Bill seemed satisfied with the answer and appeared to go back to sleep. After the service, he told us that he lived with his son and daughter-in-law, who needed a holiday, so he was only in for a week.

It was a year before we saw him again. Angela wasn't with us on that occasion, but there he was, sitting in the corner again, this time alert and very much a part of the service. Dawson asked the gathering if anyone had a testimony to give, and at once he told us that, at the service the year before, he had been moved by a young girl's testimony, and that the quality and sincerity of her reply to his question had set him thinking. After we had left that Sunday morning, he had, in the quietness, asked Jesus to come into his heart, and He had. Bill had grown so much over the year, that when he knew he was coming into the hospital again, he prayed that it would coincide with our monthly visit, and God answered his prayer! The change in him was remarkable.

One of the kitchen staff, Jean Hearn, was also a member of The Group and would often come and join us for the service. These services continued for over fifteen years.

Group Newsletter

In 1967 The Group produced its first newsletter. Photocopiers were a new thing and only the biggest firms could afford them, so for The Group it was a duplicated sheet with news about The Group and a short written testimony. In 1968 a colleague of mine gave me an old stencil duplicator, which had belonged to his father, a Baptist minister. It was very old and caked in thick dried ink. It took me about six weeks to strip it down, clean it and get it working properly. But it was well worth the effort. Because of its age, and the fact I had to stop every 50 copies or so to re-ink the rollers, the copies were not very clear. My mother had a very old 1920's typewriter, which I commandeered, and before long I was working to produce the second newsletter. The whole process of printing fascinated me, and I began a lifelong love affair with printing and publishing. Before long I had a new two-colour duplicator and a second-hand stencil scanner. Thus was born Raise Him Up Christian Publications. As well as the newsletters and service sheets, we also produced a compilation of the most popular songs and choruses that we sang. More of that under 'The Songs We Sang' later on.

Chapter 4
Other Links

Brother Francis & Beryl

One of my most treasured memories of those early days of The Group, was of the infrequent visits of Augustine to Springfield Crescent, and our equally infrequent visits to their home in Luton. They are best described by Dawson:

In the spring of 1967 Norah was heavily pregnant, carrying twins. We already had Jim (11), Christine (9) and Nick (2).

Norah was frightened about going into the large Luton and Dunstable Hospital, so a few of the Group joined me as I prayed with her. I was given a vision of two praying people, one light-skinned, the other dark.

In the hospital Norah met a light-skinned English woman, who went with her to the chapel for communion. And when I visited Norah, after the birth of the twins, there was a dark-skinned West Indian woman in the next bed, with a Christian book on her locker! It was "Peace with God" by Billy Graham. Her name was Beryl. She was from Jamaica.

When Beryl's husband came in we were soon rejoicing that the four of us were brothers and sisters in Jesus. The man's name was Augustine Francisque, known to other West Indian Christians in Luton as "Brother Francis."

We became firm friends. Occasionally Augustine came to The Group's prayer meetings. He was from St.

Lucia, where French is spoken, and his English was not always easy to understand. At one meeting he prayed at some length for "De whole wall." It was some time before we realised he was praying for the whole world!

When we first met Augustine and Beryl they were members of a Baptist church. Later they linked up with a West Indian Church led by Pastor Campbell and his wife, "Sister Campbell." They came to a meeting we held at All Saints' Church, in Harpenden, to celebrate the tenth anniversary of The Group. There was the opportunity to speak or sing in 5-minute slots. The Campbells sang, with Pastor Campbell playing the guitar. The words were simply "Jesus, Jesus, Jesus, I got you on my mind", repeated several times, ending with the line, "I got Jesus on my mind", all sung repeatedly. There was tumultuous applause when they finished.

One evening, soon after Augustine had retired from Vauxhalls, I arrived home from work at about 7pm. About 50 yards from the house I heard the sound of laughter. "I know that laugh", I thought. Sure enough it was Augustine, who had felt prompted to come and visit us. Norah conjured up a delicious meal and we had a wonderful time of fellowship together, as we always did when we met with Augustine and Beryl.

Not long afterwards Augustine died unexpectedly. There must always have been plenty of laughter in Heaven. I can imagine the great smile and the outburst of joyous laughter as he came face to face with Jesus. *D.P.*

Alice Watkins

At one point in those early days a group of young girls arrived at the prayer meeting. Who brought them I don't remember, but we soon learned that they lived in a home for girls with problems in Luton, called Koinonia[18]. Chris Williams started going out with one of the girls called Margaret, and before long we were invited to a prayer meeting at Koinonia. It was a large Victorian house built on a hill, right under the main approach path for the runway at Luton Airport.

Alice, the American lady who ran the home, was very hospitable. I shall always remember one hot evening around Whitsuntide, sitting in the front room. We were all in prayer, having just read about the day of Pentecost in Acts. Suddenly the room was filled with the sound of a mighty rushing wind and the whole house shook, as a huge jet plane skimmed the top of the house on its approach to the Airport! It was just like on the day of Pentecost.

Alice was quite strict, and I well remember on one occasion driving one of the girls home from a meeting in Harpenden. I was only dropping her off, but we were in the middle of a conversation, so we sat talking in the car for a short time, certainly not more than three minutes, when out stormed Alice, demanding that if we had anything to say to each other we could say it in the

---

18 *Koinonia* is a Greek word that occurs 20 times in the Bible. Koinonia's primary meaning is "fellowship, sharing in common, communion." The first occurrence of koinonia is Acts 2:42, "They devoted themselves to the apostles' teaching and to the fellowship, to the breaking of bread and to prayer." Christian fellowship is a key aspect of the Christian life. Believers in Christ are to come together in love, faith, and encouragement. That is the essence of koinonia.

house! I understood her concerns, though if there had been anything improper between us, I hardly think we would have sat outside her house, when there were many places to stop on the way to Luton. She was a lovely person and did a wonderful work with those girls, some of whom became Christians.

Colin Urquhart

In the early 1970s, Stewart and Carolyn Armour began to attend the Church of St. Hugh's, Lewsey Farm in Luton, where a new young vicar, the Reverend Colin Urquhart, had just taken over the parish. Colin was baptised in the Holy Spirit and was keen to see lives changed for Jesus. Very soon about a dozen of us would make the trip to their Sunday Evening Service, which, though much the same as in countless other Anglican churches, had taken on a new freedom. There was often a time for sharing during the service, and the sermons were always inspired expositions of the Word of God.

Stewart became organist there and we became good friends with many of the congregation, some of whom, including Colin, came over to The Group in Harpenden. The spiritual growth that took place in that estate church was quite phenomenal. I am sure Colin was an influencing pattern or model, on which I tried to shape my ministry.

Lorna and I began attending the Sunday Morning Eucharist there. Because of the distance involved in getting to St Hugh's, we had to set out early and often arrived half an hour or more before the services. One Sunday we arrived about 40 minutes before a

Confirmation service, to find half the congregation already praying for, and laying hands on, the candidates. Most of them received the baptism of the Holy Spirit before the Bishop even arrived!

Stewart and Carolyn joined the community at St Hugh's, which was formed before Colin left to work outside the Anglican framework[19].

The Fountain Trust

At the time of The Group, the Fountain Trust was very active, organising conferences to encourage charismatic Christians to share their experiences with their denominations and to build them up. The organisation, headed by the Reverend Michael Harper[20], brought in speakers from all over the world to speak and teach. Some of the conferences were at High Leigh Conference Centre at Hoddesdon in Hertfordshire, and many of us attended at weekends. David and Alma Pinkney were greatly involved with the Trust and made the events known to us. David started recording the talks on reel-to-reel tape recorders and making them available after the conference. He later acquired a high speed cassette tape copier, and offered cassettes about an hour after the talks ended. When the Trust organised a huge

---

19 *Colin Urquhart* laid the foundations of what has become Kingdom Faith in the late 1970's, when he moved from being an Anglican vicar in Luton to a speaker traveling the world. He is now recognized as an apostle and Kingdom Faith provides vision and direction for a growing number of churches nationally and internationally.

20 *Father Michael Harper,* Archpriest of the Antiochian Orthodox Deanery of the UK and Ireland, was born on March 12, 1931. He died of cancer on January 6, 2010, aged 78 He began his ministry in the Anglican Church but joined the Orthodox Church following the Anglican Church's decision to ordain women to the priesthood.

conference in Nottingham, with many sessions going on simultaneously, recording all the sessions required extra hands. David asked me if I would help him, so Lorna and I got to attend the conference free, in exchange for working very hard to copy and distribute each day's tapes by the following morning. It was great fun and a really wonderful experience. David and Alma were such a joy to work with. Later on David and Alma joined the Reverend Reg East, who was forming a community at Whatcombe House in Dorset.

Whatcome House is a Manor House near Winterborne Whitchurch in Dorset. In the summer of 1960, under the wardenship of Patrick Harding, it provided a stable environment for fourteen to eighteen year old maladjusted boys from around the country, in which they could gain enough self-control, self-reliance, and self-respect to be able to stand on their own two feet in the outside world. The home was funded originally by the authorities responsible for sending the boys there. Whatcombe underwent many fundamental changes in its methodology and staff, and sadly closed down in 1968 through lack of funding. Shortly after, the Reverend Reg East and a small group took it on, to operate it as a Christian Retreat house, where parish groups and individuals could find out more about Jesus and receive the baptism in the Holy Spirit or healing. Many of The Group went to Whatcombe and were greatly blessed. While David and Alma were there, they left their home in Lyndhurst Drive, in the care of Stewart Armour and his American bride, Carolyn.

At about the same time Ruth Emmett[21] won a scholarship to Dartington College of Arts[22] near Totnes in Devon, and it wasn't long before a small group of us went to the college for a weekend with her.

Those early years of the 1970's also produced a crop of weddings and a whole new generation coming to The Group.

---

21 **Ruth Fazal** née **Ennett** tells her own story, where she mentions The Group, on her website. http://www.ruthfazal.com/ruth tells her story1.htm

22 *Dartington College of Arts* was a specialist arts institution near Totnes, Devon, South West England, which specialised in post-dramatic theatre, music, performance writing and visual performance, focusing on a performative and multi-disciplinary approach to the arts. In addition to this, lecturing staff were all in some way active arts practitioners.

Chapter 5
The Next Generation

It would be easy to think that The Group was all about young people, but that was not the case; many older people came along and we saw many who, after a lifetime without God, had their lives changed. For some it was a time of recommitment. The testimonies in the second half of this book bear witness.

The Group had become a family, with old and young together. As with any gathering that involves young people, partnerships were formed and weddings took place. Indeed this was not only true of the young people; we also saw some older partnerships as well. In the space of only three years many of the younger core members of The Group were married, Bill and Betty Kemp, Ian and Maureen Cox, Martin and Lorna Hogan, David and Virginia Weston, Stewart and Carolyn Armour, Stuart and Sandy Cave, and Chris and Margaret Williams, to name but a few. Others went off to university and some emigrated.

Lorna and I stayed in Harpenden, as did Stewart and Carolyn. Others moved away but kept in touch. Most were involved in their local churches and fellowships, so the work of God continued to grow. With Dawson and Norah's family expanded to five children, it was quite a relief to them when the prayer meeting moved for a time to Martin and Lorna's new home in Coldharbour Lane. It was there that we saw a new wave of people to replace the many that had left, or were less regular as they lived further away.

Our home in Coldharbour Lane was a miracle. Lorna and I had got engaged, but had no idea where we would live or if we could afford to stay in the Harpenden area. Being a cautious type I hadn't suggested any date for getting married, as I wanted to get accommodation sorted first. We had the promise of a mortgage from the Halifax as long as I could raise a twenty percent deposit. One night as I was praying I clearly heard the Lord say, "I want you in this area, so set the date and leave the rest to Me." Lorna seemed happy with this, so we set a day just six weeks away! I thought our parents would throw a fit, but when I told mine they seemed quite happy to leave it to the Lord. I began to earnestly scan the local papers for property. Although I had almost no money at all I just knew the Lord wanted us to buy and not rent. The next Thursday morning I brought the Herts Advertiser on my way to work. I was in early, so I scanned the property adverts. One jumped out of the page at me, as though it had been printed in bold: "Two-up, two-down end of terrace cottage £5250" and a telephone number. I picked up the phone and rang straight away. "Yes you can come and see it tonight, though I warn you there are others seeing it, and one has made a tentative offer." To my amazement, I found that it was just a half mile along the road from where I worked! I arranged to view at 6pm. I telephoned Lorna and arranged to meet her outside work so we could walk along together. At 6pm we walked into the front door and fell in love with the place.

It was an end-of-terrace, two-up two-down cottage built at the end of the nineteenth century. In the late 1960s the two downstairs rooms had been knocked into one, and a bathroom toilet extension added on the ground floor, to the back of the house. The stairs to the first floor had been moved from between the two rooms to the side wall. This opened up the whole new area, making it a light and airy room. It had a rustic York stone fire place, a cedar wood sunroom extension and lots of roses in the garden. It was perfect. Before we left I made a firm offer of the asking price, although I hadn't a clue if I could raise the deposit. The owner told me he had two other couples coming to view, and a third, who had already made a tentative offer, were coming for a second visit. So if they confirmed their offer he felt he would have to let them have it. We agreed, but in our hearts we knew this was the right house. Thursday night was Bible Study night so, after a quick tea, we went along to David and Alma's home for The Group. We told them all about the house and before we started the meeting they prayed that the house would be ours. Just as we were about to begin the study, the phone rang. Alma said, "It's for you", and it was. "Martin, if you still want it, the house is yours." We left the meeting and went round immediately. The other viewers had been and gone. The couple who had made the offer and come for a second look, had tried to get the price down by verbally pulling the place to pieces. As soon as the woman started having a go at the kitchen, that was it and the owners had told them bluntly that they were obviously not interested, so they would sell to someone else. They told us that as soon as we had come to see it, they knew we would have it. So began the struggle to sort out the finances. I spent all weekend doing my sums and worrying. I was always about £1,000 short.

The following Monday I received a hand-written letter from David and Alma, saying that God had told them He wanted Lorna and me in the area for some time to come, and that they were to make available to us a sum of money, with no strings attached: They didn't know how much it would be, but it could be as much as £1,000. Wow! That was a lot of money in 1971!

The transaction progressed and we got married, and lived for a few weeks in Lorna's rented bedsit. Then at last the day came for us to pay the deposit and complete. I was exactly £780 short. On the morning I was due to pay the solicitor the money, a cheque arrived through the post from David and Alma for the exact amount! I went straight to the bank to pay it in, and to ask for special clearance as I needed to pay it out straight away. The cashier told me that as it was a cheque drawn on the same bank and branch as mine they could clear it immediately at no charge! So we were able to place the money into the solicitor's hands just in time. The Lord is good. The day we moved into the cottage I borrowed a van from work and drove around to all the people who had promised us bits of furniture, and that night we had a fully furnished home, where we stayed for seven years.

The area under the stairs, which was in the kitchen, provided a sort of annex to the sitting room, and gave us enough space on prayer meeting nights, to add another chair into the circle. Soon after we started hosting the meeting, we were all gathered for prayer, and one of our older regular members was sitting under the stairs. Suddenly, without provocation, she had an outburst of anger, quite out of character, which for a time shattered the peace and harmony in the room. She later said that she didn't know what had come over her; she had been perfectly relaxed and nothing was troubling her. It had just seized her. Later that week I called together some of The Group to pray over the house for us. 'Old Bill', who had not been at the prayer meeting, told us that he could have told us that, some years before, someone had committed suicide in the house, by putting her head in a gas oven, which had been situated just where the woman was sitting! We spent a considerable time praying over the whole house, cleansing it from any dark or evil influences from the past. During that time of prayer, Stewart had a vision of a snake slithering from under the stairs and out of the front door. We never had any more trouble, and after that many people, including a large number of young people from the Church Youth Group, which I had recently started, gave their hearts to Jesus and were baptised in the Holy Spirit in that room.

Peter and Liz Heywood

One evening I had a telephone call from a Company Director of a Robotics firm, who had been referred to us by the Fountain Trust. He was shortly to be transferred to our area and had enquired of the Trust what charismatic groups there were nearby. He was coming down the following week to view properties and would like to meet us. We invited him to stay with us and there began a friendship, which has lasted for nearly 40 years. Peter and Liz Heywood moved to Wheathampstead and started a fellowship there. We lost touch for two years while I went to Theological College in the early 80s. In November 1984 I visited the parish of Holy Trinity, St Austell in Cornwall, to consider becoming their curate. In our tour of the parish we called in at the Christian Coffee Shop run by a couple from the church. They told us that another couple had just moved into a manor house on the Roseland Peninsular, and were opening it as a Christian holiday centre. Apparently they knew us and could we get in touch? It was Peter and Liz! We soon met up with them, and often visited them at that remarkable centre, Trewince Manor[23].

The Lord recently (2009) showed me a vision of a tapestry being woven. He showed me how one thread can crop up many times in different parts of the tapestry. He went on to tell me that relationships in life are like that. No encounter is isolated and no meeting is by chance. Like Dawson and Norah, Peter and Liz have been with us, sometimes at crucial decision making times, and we have always been grateful for their fellowship, friendship and counsel, which all started with The Group.

Reverend Paul Hutchinson

In the mid seventies one of our regular members was the Reverend Paul Hutchinson, who was the vicar of St. Mary's Anglican Church, Marshalswick, in St. Albans. Paul came into the baptism of the Holy Spirit while at

---

23 *Trewince Manor* website: http://www.trewince.co.uk/home

Marshalswick, and it transformed his ministry and his preaching. He shared his experience with some of the senior members of his congregation, but they didn't understand what had happened to him, and kindly suggested that he should see a counsellor or psychiatrist! Paul took refuge in The Group, where he was understood and supported. Although he attended fairly regularly, he rarely said much, preferring to sit and soak in the love and presence of the Lord. He became a good friend and encouragement to me. On the rare occasions when we felt the leading to break bread together, he would enthusiastically take part, but never took a leading role.

Sister Audrey Mary

In the early seventies a group of Anglican nuns purchased a small block of flats in Milton Road, which they opened as a rehabilitation centre for women drug addicts. It was called Spelthorne St Mary's. As well as their work with the young women, the sisters were involved in the work of the parish church. It was through their involvement with the parish that Sister Audrey Mary heard about The Group, and asked if she could come along. We were delighted, and welcomed her with open arms. She was a wise, gentle and very loving lady who had received the baptism in the Holy Spirit some years before coming to Harpenden, but had not enjoyed like-minded fellowship since. The Group became a spiritual sanctuary for her, and she in turn gave much of her own spiritual insight and learning to us. She was greatly used in the gift of prophecy, and when we had our first child, prophesied that Lorna would have an abundance of motherhood! That certainly came true and we now have five children, who in turn are producing families. Although in her late fifties at the time, Sister Audrey Mary had a sparkle of youth about her and was always full of laughter and fun. What none of us knew at the time, because she never let on, was that she was dying of cancer, and was often in great pain. What a witness she was to us all.

Changing Patterns

Over the next few years The Group went through several 'ups' and 'downs'. From the highs of the early seventies, at times we went down to a mere dozen, and at other times of being up in the twenties again. From being mostly young, unchurched people, we went through times of having few, if any, young people, just older and more regular churchgoers. It mattered little. What was important was that we were there for whoever came, and that we remained faithful in our prayer, and our belief in the authority of the Word of God. In the mid seventies, while Lorna was busy with babies, we changed the pattern of the Bible study meetings by meeting at different locations. Maysie hosted one meeting a month for a number of years. After Maysie died, Dawson and Norah bought her bungalow and moved in there while their newly married daughter Christine, moved into Springfield Crescent. Before I left The Group in 1983, to go to college and train for the ministry, The Group returned to Dawson and Norah's home and continued to thrive as a once-a-week Bible study and prayer group. Dawson retired from the UKAEA where he was a

Personnel Director, and trained for ordination at Oak Hill. The group continued throughout his training, with Rosemary Hill sharing the leadership with him. After he was ordained in 1991, he gave the parish of St Nicholas Harpenden ten years until he retired to St Thomas, Fair Oak, Hampshire. Rosemary wrote to me in March 2011 and made the following comments:

Dawson and Norah's Home Fellowship Group was a time of peace after what could be a difficult week. It was a joy to pray with other 'prayers', to feel free to pray as God led, and to know that anybody new who came along had been brought by God (via Dawson or Norah!) so the prayers would be inclusive for them.

The Bible study was also inspired by God. I can remember so many times that we wrestled with a passage bringing out painful memories, which were then healed, or preparing someone for a trial that was to come, a trial God knew was coming but that we could have no idea was on the horizon.

Most of my special memories also include someone else, so I would rather not go into detail. Just say how wonderful it was to have God working every week during the meeting. R.H.

Dawson's influence on members of The Group was tremendous. We all held him in the highest esteem and will always be grateful that he has spent his life listening to God and passing on the guidance he received. I was the first of The Group members to respond to the call to ordination. I'm sure I would not have done so without his wisdom and encouragement urging me on. Much later on, long after I had left, another member of The Group, Rosemary's young son Ian, responded to God's call to ordination, and again Dawson's influence was apparent. Ian writes:

Soon after University in the early 1990s I had a temporary job, but because of the recession was struggling to find a permanent position, so that became one of the things we prayed about in the Friday night prayer group. Unknown to anyone else, I was also wrestling with God at the time; I felt He was calling me into ordained stipendiary ministry in the Church of England – something I resolutely didn't want to do! Slowly God graciously demolished my arguments, until I was left with just one: "I want, without prompting, independent confirmation from somebody who I respect, preferably Dawson Price, telling me that I should be ordained". Eventually God persuaded me that if He called me, I didn't need anyone else to confirm it; His call was enough. Once I gave in, I felt God saying "Great, I've got a marker on your life now, I'll tell you when I want you to act on it". Within a week of that I was offered a permanent job. I arrived early that Friday and told Norah and Dawson the good news. "But I'm not sure I'll be there for my whole career", I said, to which Dawson responded, "No, neither am I". Pressed as to why (I have never seen Dawson find it so hard to say something before or since), he blurted out, "Because I think you will be ordained one day," and I am! I.H.

Let us not forget Norah either, who would often get talking to people while walking the dog, and would bring their needs to The Group for prayer, or would bring the un-churched, non-christian to the meetings, who often returned again and again.

After his own ordination in 1991, Dawson spent most of his energy serving the parish of St Nicholas,

Harpenden, especially through the Family Service, which grew tremendously during that time. His wisdom and his experience in handling people were greatly used and valued in the parish and beyond.

The Group ran continuously for thirty-four years. In those thirty-four years the Lord has used The Group to launch hundreds, yes hundreds, of people of all ages, on to a closer walk with Jesus. Dozens have been called into full-time or part-time ministry, ordained and lay, like Jimmy Kendal, who felt the leading of the Lord to give up his job in Harpenden and work for fourteen years with the Vietnamese boat people in Hong Kong.

I have in my possession a listing of all those who came to The Group over a fifteen year period. It contains the names of well over eight hundred people of all ages! If all the testimonies of those eight hundred people were to be written down, it would require a book much bigger than this one, to record them all in! In the second half of this book are recorded just a few of those testimonies, mostly from the early years. Some of the names, like Ruth Fazal, you may recognise, as she now has a world-wide ministry in music. Some of them have now passed on from this life and are now enjoying the nearer presence of the Lord. Some have very kindly sent me updates, for which I am very grateful. As I read these testimonies again, and as I run my eyes down the list of names, my heart is filled with thankfulness that the Lord allowed me to be a part of His great work in The Harpenden Group.

Part 2
Testimonies

When people became Christians in The Group, they were encouraged to share their story and to acknowledge the hand of God in their lives. Many of them kindly wrote their stories down. Some were published in The Group Newsletter, some in the Parish Magazine, and some just kept by Dawson in a folder labelled The Group. I have also included articles from the local Church Magazine by members of The Group, contributing to a series called 'Why I believe in God.'

They are not in any order of preference. I have grouped together those by the same person. Unless otherwise stated, they were all written down in the late 60's early 70's.

DAWSON PRICE

Why I Believe in God - 1967

To explain why I believe in God, I have to go back to the starting point of my belief, over seventeen years ago. My parents were not churchgoers. I had been to church once or twice out of curiosity, but I had found nothing either to attract me or challenge me. I was a convinced atheist, absolutely certain that God was just a figment of the imagination of people who found it comforting to think that way. So I had gone to university, confident in my atheistic beliefs.

At the university, I came across other students, who were convinced Christians and were not afraid to talk about their faith as the most important thing in their lives. I had quite a few talks with them, and they listened with good humour and patience to all my arguments. I learned later that, as well as discussing their faith with me, they were also praying for me.

Two things made me willing to listen to these students. One was that, for some time, I had been wondering whether there was any purpose in life. The other was that they seemed to have something I knew I lacked. It would be difficult to define exactly what it was, but it was a blend of peace, certainty, enthusiasm, power, joy and the capacity for really caring about other people.

I went with them to church. It was the first time I had seen a full church, and the first time I had heard Christianity preached in a way that was relevant to my own life. I was made aware of God's love, of my free choice to love Him or not, of my love for self rather than God leading to all the sin of my life, of total forgiveness through the cross of Christ, of the clean start and new life offered by Jesus, and of His willingness to come into my life and strike up a personal relationship with me, if only I would ask him.

For a while I fought against all this, in my mind. It might make differences in my life which would not be convenient. Finally, I was given a copy of John's gospel, with the suggestion that I should read it straight through like a story. I did. I was so drawn to Jesus as I read about Him that my opposition melted. I went to the church again and talked afterwards to one of the convinced

Christians, who prayed with me. After he had left, I knelt by my bed and quite simply asked the Lord Jesus Christ to come into my life.

Now I can say that I believe in God because I have found that it works. What I had read about in the Bible has come true in experience. I know that when I am praying I am not just talking to the empty air, because prayers have been answered, often in ways totally inexplicable in purely human terms.

NORAH PRICE

I always felt very forlorn and terribly unhappy as a little girl, and very aware of my misery and fear. Nothing and nobody ever made me feel secure. My family was poor, very loving, and we all stuck together. When I look back and compare, I realise my criticism of my parents was unfair, but young people are sure they could do better.

When I was about eleven, we were all asked, as was the custom in a Church of England school, to be confirmed. When my mother said, "You can't be confirmed; you haven't been christened," my heart dropped into my boots as usual. I told the head teacher and he said, "We had better not shame your parents, so you can't be done." Looking back, I know that this sad time was wonderfully used by the Lord. I just asked Jesus into my life by christening myself in our little stream. I know now that God honoured that. I must admit that I felt it probably couldn't count, and how I hated the lack of concern in the grown-up hearts.

I went to Secondary School at thirteen, much to my amazement. I remember the next three years as the happiest in my life so far. I knew Dawson in those years. I loved the O-level work, except the maths. Then the 1944 Education Act abolished my school, and my form of twenty-one pupils had to take O-level two years early! It was School Certificate in those days, and we had to pass a minimum of six subjects. I only passed four subjects and therefore failed. I've never felt so miserable in my life. I had prayed to pass my School Certificate. What a mess! What was I going to do? I walked along the river bank and prayed and thought of drowning myself. My mother's hackles were up because we had been cheated.

I was packed off to the High School to try again. At the end of that year I passed ten subjects, but it didn't matter much, as O-levels had come in then. What did matter was that I had met Miss Southam, the Christian head at the Girls High School. She was hated by most empty-headed girls, but I'd never liked anyone like that until now. She encouraged and taught me so much. Her assemblies were terrific, full of Christian teaching, hymns and Bible reading. I can remember kneeling in my gym slip, two and a half inches above the floor, drinking in the food for my soul. I went to my own village church occasionally. I didn't belong at all. It is still just as deadly now when I go back. I did a year's A-level work mixed with a general sixth year, really just kicking my heels until I got into Teacher Training College.

In my last fortnight at school, Dawson came back on the scene. He was reading history at Cambridge by then. He didn't seem to take much notice of me and talked to some of the lads. I thought, "I love him. I'd like to marry him." My mother still says I threw my satchel in and said, "I won't need that, I'm going to get married!" She was great at taking my wild statements, wonderful through the teenage struggles, marvellous at trusting us, and honest about everything. I am sure now her own desire for some food for her soul was as real as my own, but she might as well have been in darkest Africa! She couldn't have been further away from the gospel of Jesus Christ. We sported a Bible and a few Jehovah's Witness volumes. They were as alive as a bucket of coal to us.

Dawson *had* realised I existed and asked me out, with him and his friend. We wrote to each other during my first year at Training College. I roomed with Monica, who was a Baptist. She was shining for Jesus, just like the chorus says. My College Mother was a Christian. I joined the Christian Union with Monica. Bless her, she even invited me to a weekend house party. I never went to one of those. However I was really drawn to her way of life and I went to a rally in the Albert Hall. Tom Rees was preaching, and he told us about Noah trusting God, and how Jesus died for me and that He wanted me to ask him into my life. If I wanted Him in, I was to stand up. I did! I've never wanted anything so much in my life, or seemed to wait so long for it. Tom Rees said, "Go back and kneel beside your bed and say your prayers." Wow! In that room with five girls! They never batted an eyelid. I wrote to tell Dawson. Praise the Lord, he had been converted the same week in Cambridge, and he wrote to tell me!

I joined the C. of E. and was christened and confirmed in Dawson's village with him. My sister was taking R.C. instruction at the same time. Dawson and I were married. We have always given the Lord Jesus first claim on our lives. It has been pretty wonderful and has become more so as we have allowed Him more of our lives. It is most exciting. It is seventeen years ago now. These years are a different story.

BILL KEMP - February 2011

The Beginning

Our van came to a halt at a set of traffic lights next to a large poster advertising a religious crusade. My friend commented, 'I'd like to go to that, but I'm afraid of being converted.' If I was truthful to myself, I felt exactly the same way, but these were words that I would come to remember, as being a landmark moment in my life.

We were returning home from Brands Hatch Racing Circuit with our racing motorcycles. At the age of 22 my overriding desire in life was to race motorcycles. Every weekend in the summer months we would attend races all over the country. Nothing could equal the thrill and excitement, which I experienced on the race circuit, so the thought of going to church did not interest me in the slightest.

For the previous few weeks I had been seated next to a man at work, who had been telling me the story of how he came to faith in Jesus Christ. I listened to him and could tell that something genuine had happened, that changed the focus of his life. But I had dismissed his experience as being irrelevant to my lifestyle. Although the words of Jesus he had quoted to me remained in my mind, I managed to satisfy myself that I was young and had plenty of time to consider them when I was older.

We are never satisfied with the things we have, and I was no different. Bigger, better, faster, was the urge that drove us. So my friend bought a new bike, which cost him all that he had and more beside. He was really looking forward to his first race on his new machine, which held great promise for him. The first time he raced on it was to prove a day I shall never forget.

The weather was fine at Oulton Park racing circuit. He went out for his first ride of the day, and when he failed to appear the first time round, I began to wonder what had happened to him. The ambulance was sent out when the race finished, and upon its return I looked in, to see him lying there, pale and lifeless. The medics were working on him, trying to find a response in his reflexes, but to no avail. At that moment the words of Jesus Christ came flooding back into my mind. Death had seemed a lifetime away, but now my friend, who was only 18 years old, lay dead on the stretcher in the ambulance.

Two days later, in the early hours of the morning, I was to experience something that I had never felt before. I was on my own, thinking about going to bed, when suddenly I felt the presence of Somebody, whom I could not see, in the room with me! I was scared, as this was something outside my experience, so tried to escape from it. All night long I felt the presence there. I had to find out what was happening, so the next morning I went to see the man who told me about Jesus Christ. Surely he could help me. What he said to me stirred something within me. He explained that if Jesus Christ rose from the dead, He must be alive, and that it was His presence I had felt all night. He was bringing me to the place where I would give my life to Him. Gradually the truth about the futility of my life began to dawn on me, so finding a place on my own, I asked Jesus Christ to come into my life and forgive my sin.

I soon discovered that Jesus is alive, because He changed my life immediately. It was like being a new person. A weight that I had been carrying around on my shoulders for years suddenly seemed to roll off, and I was free. I had a new purpose and an excitement that I had never known before. All the fear of death vanished, because everything I had been told about the Lord Jesus was true.

What Next

From that moment on my overwhelming desire was to be filled with the Holy Spirit. It was with great excitement that I heard about a Billy Graham follow-up meeting, to be held in the home of a local Anglican Lay Reader. So I decided to go to his house beforehand to check him out. I had heard that no one in the Anglican Church could possibly be a true Christian, therefore, bristling with all my new found zeal, I went to 'sort him out' with the 'real truth'. Dawson opened the door, and I began to pour out the things I now considered to be all that was essential to real faith in Jesus Christ.

Every statement was met with a gracious response. "Yes," he replied, "that's what I believe." As we spoke, I felt my aggression melt away, and as I came to my last statement, "I want to be filled the Holy Spirit," a bond was forged between us. He invited me in, and from that moment on I knew we were of the same mind and the same spirit.

The Bible Study Started

For the first year, numbers remained low. Week by week we went through the Billy Graham Crusade follow-up Bible Study notes, but although these were excellent, somehow we needed a spark of life. This was to come when, after a year, a Crusade follow-up rally was organised in the centre of Harpenden. At this meeting we were to meet Marion, a teenage girl, who had originally been referred to the Bible studies, but had not felt that they would interest her. However, after some encouragement and the offer of a lift to the meetings, she decided to give it a go. From my recollection, her arrival was like a spark that set the fire blazing. Her enthusiasm and excitement was contagious, and within what seemed a short space of time, she began to bring along her school friends, and they in turn brought their friends.

Soon numbers were swelling and Dawson's lounge was fast becoming too small for the meetings! As we got to the point of wondering what we could do, God answered our prayer. David and Alma, who had been referred to Dawson by The Fountain Trust, arrived at the meeting and offered their much larger lounge to host the Bible Study. Even this venue eventually became too small, and the meeting had to be split into two, with one group meeting in an upstairs room! This was now the pattern that was followed for each of the Bible Study meetings. We would all start together with a time of worship and then split into two groups for the study. Afterwards we joined together again for refreshments and fellowship.

The Prayer Meeting

When the Prayer Meeting first started we were still meeting in Dawson and Norah's house. Their family had now expanded to five children (two of them babies). Both Dawson and Norah must have been under great stress. Looking back on those times, I am still amazed at their love and grace towards the number of people who invaded their home twice a week. If they did suffer times of tiredness or stress, they never showed it to us. If a seat in Heaven could be reserved for me, it would be next to Dawson and Norah because their seats would surely be in a place of honour!

The Prayer Meeting continued to be held in the same place and grew quickly. From time to time we had special meetings for specific prayer. Included in these meetings were times when we would receive ministry for the baptism in the Holy Spirit, and it was on one of these occasions that I received the fullness of the Spirit. Once again it was to be an Anglican Minister who would pray for me. His ministry is still vivid in my mind, as he prayed, shared and encouraged us to reach out and submit to the Lord, and the Holy Spirit came upon me and loosened my stammering tongue. Praise and prayer poured out in what I can only describe as a 'Pentecostal' experience, a language that I did not understand and certainly had never learned. This was to prove an invaluable help and strengthened me in my walk with the Lord. From that time on Jesus somehow became closer, and though difficult to describe, became even more real to me.

One outstanding moment was on the occasion of a visit from a lady, who had in her time been a missionary to a remote tribe somewhere in Africa. David, who was by this time virtually blind, always lived with his mother and had certainly never been to Africa, started praying in tongues. Suddenly this lady became excited, and wanted to know how he could speak so fluently in a language that, as far as she knew, was unknown outside this same remote tribe! He had apparently been praising the Lord and praying for his mother.

Ever heard the phrase, 'Don't go near those Pentecostal charismatic meetings, they roll about on the floor and swing on chandeliers...?' Well, I never saw such behaviour, but we certainly got excited sometimes. What the neighbours thought was going on in Dawson's house on a Tuesday can only be imagined! How Dawson and Norah faced them the next day is a mystery to me. One evening I had to leave the meeting early, about 9 pm while it was still in full swing. I walked about fifty yards down the road and turned the corner, where I could still hear the praise and worship going on!

The Prayer time started at 8pm and we tried to finish by 9.30pm, but there were times when that proved difficult, since so many were still engaged in prayer. After eventually coming to a stop and refreshments had been served, Dawson would get his house back as late as

11pm. Early next morning he would once again be commuting to his high profile job in London.

Dawson and Norah were far too gracious and humble to acknowledge that, but for them and their faithfulness, dedication, counsel, friendship and love, many of us would wonder if we would be where we are today. They were truly to me a father and mother in the faith.

Other Activities

It was always accepted that The Harpenden Prayer Group would never become a church. However, that did not stop some of the younger people wanting to go to church on Sunday evenings. I purchased a large six-seat car, and we would go to an Apostolic Pentecostal Church on Sunday evenings. Although only a small elderly congregation, they welcomed us with open arms, and encouraged us with opportunities to share and testify to our faith. The minister would invite us back to his house after the service, for fellowship and refreshments. This car saw many journeys to and from the meetings, picking up people and bringing them home again. Three times a week, I would start from Harpenden, drive to Hatfield to pick up Pete, then to St Albans, and continue on via Sandridge back to Harpenden to collect people for the Meetings. One evening on the return journey with the car full, we were approaching a junction at a crossroad, which had a central reservation, when, although we had the right of way, a car coming in the opposite direction turned right to pass in front of us. I had no time to think and react, but the steering wheel turned sharply to the right as if by an unseen hand, and our two cars passed each other on the junction.The rear bumpers just touched, without causing any damage! Both cars stopped and we were able to go and see the other driver, who was shaken, but unharmed. We shared with her how God had protected us.

The car became too small, so I obtained a twelve seat minibus. This would enable us to carry more people to go to special meetings and to travel to nearby towns on Saturday nights to witness to others about our faith. One year a group of us went to the Apostolic Church Convention in South Wales. It was as if this period of our life would go on for ever.

The Beginning of Change

University and careers were now beginning to become important for many of the younger people. Gradually they left to pursue the next stage of their lives, and The Group began to take on a different dynamic.

The Lord spoke to me and told me that my time in The Group was coming to an end. I shared this with Dawson, and he said, "Bill, I will tell you what the Lord has said to me. Within a year you will no longer be with us; you will have moved on." Within a year I had met my wife, got married and moved away to another town and to different ministries.

The Group was to continue for many years to come. Different people came and carried on the Lord's work, but the same ethos and vision was maintained, introducing people to Jesus and leading them into the fullness of the Spirit.

Now, after forty years, I can look back at those extraordinary years which laid the foundations for the rest of my life. During these years Betty and I have been involved in many Christian churches, ministries and activities. Standing out from all these are those early years of The Harpenden Group. Many people came to faith and matured in their Christian lives, giving us memorable fellowship and leaving us with a wealth of happy memories.

My special thanks must go to Dawson and Norah, who by their faithful love made it all possible. Our sincere appreciation goes to Martin who has provided us with the opportunity to share our memories, and remind us how blessed we were to be part of this move of God's Holy Spirit.

JACQUIE WEBB

It was last year, 1966, just before the Billy Graham Crusade, when I first heard about Jesus Christ. My boyfriend had just changed jobs, and by a series of circumstances was seated next to a Christian who started witnessing to him. In turn, it came back to me. We tried at first to work out when the end of the world was coming, not worrying about our souls at all. Then one day a friend of Bill's was killed on the race track. It was through that, that Bill asked the Lord Jesus Christ into his life.

On 7th June 1966 we both went to the Billy Graham Crusade. After Billy Graham had given the message, there was something inside me saying, "Go forward", so I did. I was very nervous, not knowing what I was letting myself in for. Nevertheless I went. That, praise the Lord, wasn't the end. My boyfriend and I had loads of rows, mostly about Jesus. Every time he started talking about Jesus, I thought, "There he goes again." Ever been cheesed off? Well I was, every time. I just wished he would go away and leave me alone, but he didn't. By Christmas I finally thought, "I am not a Christian any more". I talked to Bill about it and got nowhere. I talked to Norah and Dawson and still didn't seem to find the answer. One night in January, after coming home on the train from work, I was feeling so fed up. Bill came round for me, and we went to pick up some tracts from Arthur Milton. On the way back, Bill kept saying things that were true about me. At first I was just rejecting it all and fighting it. But there is no fighting Jesus. When He is there, He is really there. When we got back to my place I prayed a prayer in my heart, that if the Lord really did want me, He would show me something in the Bible. He did; it was Psalm 20. On Saturday night, January 22nd I let Jesus into my life for good, and now praise His wonderful name for saving my soul from hell. From that day to this, I have known the Lord, His peace, love and goodness, and He is with me all the time, both day and night.

I thank the Lord for giving me the Bible Study. If it hadn't been for that, and people praying for me, I don't know where I would be now, so Praise the Lord. Amen.

DAVID PINKNEY

Born 1912 - Reborn 1st August 1967!

I was trained as a physicist never to believe what could not be proved by argument or experiments. Alma, who married me, brought me into contact with the Oxford Group in 1935. I agreed with the 'standards' but not the surrender. Why must I surrender my right of criticism? All I had to do was to live to Christian rules.

I went into the Control Instrument business and did well, but in 1962 I realised I had lost all my enthusiasm (almost a breakdown). I had guidance with Alma, resigned my job and we planned to emigrate to Australia. I even got a job there. A few weeks later I was told I'd got T.B. on the kidney. I had 6 months in hospital doing nothing (which I enjoyed) and God, through a good friend, gave me a very little bit of faith. I also got cured but was refused entry to Australia for two years.

I listened to God for guidance, and I was led to a new job, which I plunged into and nearly had another breakdown. However, God was holding me in spite of myself. Alma and I went to the Fountain Trust holiday week at High Leigh. I was terrified that if I surrendered to God, he would want me to chuck in my job and become a missionary or something utterly strange to me. But someone said, "God is your father. Would you not trust your father to be gentle with you? Trust Him."

I was most moved by Reg East's evening talk on coming to Jesus and letting Him break you. In guidance God had told me, "Stop trying to deal only with the Chairman. You go and talk to my Personnel Officer". So I went to Jesus. I asked him to break me, to show me myself as I really was, and then to help me face it. He did, and I wept with relief and joy. Alma had a similar experience, and we came to each other through the gift the Lord had given to each of us. It was wonderful!

Fortunately the Lord grabbed me by the scruff of the neck, just as I was ready to tell everybody what idiots they were and to try to give them the gift the Lord gave to me! He said, "That gift is for you from me - you must not try to give it away. I will tell you what to do, and who you may help bring to Me." And so I was saved, and learned, not to be God's engineer, but to read and listen to the Word and to want joyously to do God's will. Every time I fall flat on my face, I know who will rescue me when I ask Him. I don't try to be a Christian - I tell the Lord I want to be a Christian. I know I can do nothing worthwhile in my own strength. By surrendering my freedom to the Lord, He has made me free and alive. Hallelujah!

DAVID PINKNEY

Why I Believe in God

Science cannot prove that God exists, nor can science prove that God does not exist.   On this problem, science isn't any help at all. I am a scientist, so I ought to know. If you believe that the world or "energy and mass" was created, then the creator is called God. If you do not believe in a creator, then you are left trying to put into words something beyond human understanding. So let's say that God created everything, and so is greater than all His creations, including men and women.

Now, for me, men and women first happened when the creatures concerned first thought about nonmaterial things, like good and evil, right and wrong and love and hate. As soon as they did, they came up against the problem of "choosing". It is rather nicely described in the story of Adam and Eve. They made the wrong choice. Don't we all! So the next job was to train Man to behave himself and to make the right choices. The Ten Commandments and the Law set out the rules for the Jews, who were spiritually the most advanced nation of their age. The first was to worship and love God. If you kept the rules you would prosper. It didn't work too well, because whenever the Jews prospered, that very prosperity brought greed, pride, corruption, cruelty, oppression and finally collapse - to be repeated many times.

So God became man: a real man, not God play-acting a man. Jesus claimed to be that man. What a pointless and outrageous claim if it was not true! So easy to prove untrue. One real fault, one real sin, one false statement - and Bingo! - the claim fails. But it didn't fail. I believe it is true.

But what marvellous "good news" Jesus brought us! He said, "If a man loves me, he will keep my word, and my Father will love him, and we will come to him and make our home with him." What a message of joy! You have only to see what this, and more "good news" did to the early Christians, after the authorities, Church and State, had executed their leader, Jesus. Jesus really did come and make His home in their hearts, and they set the world aflame. Jesus made His home in my heart five months ago, when, in my utter feebleness, I asked Him to. God can deal with any problem in my life if I take it to Jesus. The only fear I need to retain is that I shall lose touch with Him.

If you have not already done it, you too can choose to believe in God, to love God, to want to do His will, to take yourself and your load to Jesus, to have His love and forgiveness and to receive the joy and courage to enjoy life to the full. I hope you do.

You can choose to do none of these things. God never compels; He only beckons.

ALMA PINKNEY

I was brought up with a mixed Christian background - having a Presbyterian father, a C of E mother and having attended Sunday School at the Congregational Church nearby.

When I was 18, my sister, as a 'cub reporter' on the Bournemouth Times, was sent to Oxford to investigate the House Parties that were taking place there; thousands of people from all over the country were gathering to hear about the way the Lord was working in individual lives. This was the great revival of my generation. (early 1930's) My sister was won, decided to let the Lord run her life and sent for my mother and me to go and learn about it. I didn't want to go, but we went, and at the end of a week the Lord had spoken to me, and I knew that this was the "putting into practice" the things we'd heard about in church Sunday by Sunday. It meant extricating myself from a wrong relationship and making restitution where possible, apologising to my mother and various other things. Our whole family, father, mother, sister and I, accepted this Oxford Group way of living.

During that year, 1934 to 35, the Lord used me to bring others to Him. But the seed must have fallen on poor soil, because at the end of the year a young man asked me to marry him, and faced with the choice of saying no to him or no to the Lord, I turned away from the Lord and got married.

The Lord didn't let me go - and eleven years later a girl, whom the Lord had used me to change at College in 1934, was the instrument the Lord chose to bring me back to Himself. She had remained faithful, and in 1946 she arranged for me to go and stay for a week in Devon, where a great Christian woman brought me to the foot of the Cross, and made me see my own sin and what it was doing to others. Again I committed my life to the Lord, accepting His daily guidance, checked by the four absolute standards of honesty, purity, unselfishness and love, and moreover by other trusted friends who had likewise committed their lives to God. This time it meant asking forgiveness of my husband, putting right what I could and making restitution where possible. This time it meant groping back from unbelief. It meant saying "Oh God, IF you exist ....".

The Lord was a wonderful loving Father, even in my blindness and confusion. He was so gentle and gave me good Christian friends to help me along.

In 1952 my sister and I spent a week at Lee Abbey, in North Devon, and on the last evening there, we went together into the chapel with "Pop" (one of the Community there, who had helped us both) and knelt down and audibly asked the Lord Jesus into our lives. I remember feeling radiant in the train going home next day, and feeling that up to that point I had been putting the cart before the horse. I had been struggling to put right what was wrong in my own life and help others to do the same, instead of asking the Lord Jesus Christ to carry the load and do it for me.

When my sister died in 1961, a radiant witness to Christ, the Lord gave me a great blessing - a very real and living presence of Himself. So I tried to serve Him more completely, but still did not know Him as my personal Saviour, and during these last two or three years I knew that I was a compromising Christian, and lacked the joy and peace that Christ promised to all who were His.

This summer, David and I spent a week at a Holiday Conference at High Leigh, and during that week, David asked the Lord Jesus into his heart. I experienced a rebirth - one of those glimpses of Heaven that the Lord permits from time to time. When I went to High Leigh, I was hoping for something wonderful to happen, but I had no real faith that it would. The Lord poured His riches and blessing on us, in a way I had never even imagined! He showed me so clearly the depth of my own sin against Him, and how I nailed Him to His cross, treated Him with contempt and contributed to His crown of thorns with my selfishness and self-will. And yet His blood cleanses me from all these sins. He washed me clean, and poured His love in and gave me the deepest desires of my heart in abundant riches. David and I were both filled with love for Him, and it overflowed, in new love for each other - He transformed our marriage; after 50 years we were like newlyweds!

I think my story is like the story of Abraham, and up to going to High Leigh this summer, my God was the God of the Old Testament. However, from August 1967 I know the fullness and the joy of loving the God of the New Testament, the loving Father who came Himself to give His blood, to save me and cleanse me from my sins.

We just keep saying, "Isn't the Lord wonderful?" and "Praise the Lord!"

ALMA PINKNEY

Why I Believe in God

I believe in God because He is real - He is there.

Both my parents hailed from Northern Ireland and I am by nature a gambler. Twenty-one years ago, I gambled my whole life on the reality of God. He has never failed, I cried out to Him then, "Oh God, if You exist - tell me what to do!" Instantly the answer came, "If you want to know Me, read the Bible." Nothing else. I could not find a Bible in our flat, but after some searching I finally came up with a Moffatt's Translation of the New Testament, so I started on that. It was full of the most moving stories. Mirrored there, I saw myself and God's loving answer to my deepest needs, through Jesus Christ. I saw Him meeting the needs of people I knew, who were just the same kind of people who met Him and were met by Him in Jerusalem and Galilee, nearly 2,000 years earlier.

At that time I had to do my Bible reading, and getting to know Him, between 5:30 and 6:30am, before the day began. Like Elijah, I found the Lord in the still, small voice. That still small voice, would speak to me at all sorts of unexpected times. As I came to recognise His voice I also learned to step out into the unknown in faith. Although it often seemed to me like stepping over an immense precipice into space, when I took the step I found firm ground always miraculously there.

God is always there, if we really mean business about wanting to know Him.

I suppose, being a natural gambler, it was easier for me to stake everything time and time again - but with this difference - I never lost! I know now, that this is not a gamble; it's a winner, it's a certainty!

DAVID AND ALMA PINKNEY

In July 1967, David and I went to a holiday conference at High Leigh, Hoddesden, arranged by the Fountain Trust. Our friends of over twenty years standing, the Reverend Reg and Mrs. Lucia East, were host and hostess, backing up the Reverend Michael and Mrs. Jeanne Harper. Michael was the secretary of The Fountain Trust. Visiting speakers were Campbell McAlpine, and David Smith of St. Mark's Church, Gillingham, Kent. During that week many miracles took place amongst those assembled - and the most wonderful one for us was something I had prayed and longed for, for many years; David accepted Jesus Christ into his heart as his Saviour and Lord! He became a Christian. For me this was the most incredible miracle! The Lord performed quite a spiritual operation on me too, opening my blind spiritual eyes and showing me the Lord, Jesus Christ, as MY Saviour. We were two new people.

Our friends, the Easts, had known that we were searching and seeking for some time, and had invited us to many meetings in London the previous winter, arranged by Michael Harper, where David du Plessis had been speaking. They had also sent us the address of a Christian couple in Harpenden. But we were not ready and didn't respond. When I saw Lucia at High Leigh, I apologised for not following up her lead and calling on the couple. She cheerfully said it might have been for the best as they had now left Harpenden, but she had the name and address of another couple, now in Harpenden, who had been baptised in the Holy Spirit. She gave me their details, and this time, without more ado, we called on them on the day we got back home. This couple were Dawson and Norah Price.

It was a Sunday evening and they welcomed us warmly. After one look at our radiant faces, they suggested that we come to their prayer meeting the following Tuesday evening, which we did. There were six others there, apart from the Prices. We later met Bill Kemp and his friend, who had been on holiday. I had been praying for real Christian fellowship for some time, and it was a joy when the Lord brought us together. I got to know Norah well, and I was thrilled to help her once a week with her baby twins, and to release her for visits to the dentist.

Earlier that summer there had been a Billy Graham Crusade, culminating in a special week in St. Albans, which attracted many young people. Several joined our meetings, and numbers grew to sixteen. Two evenings a week producing sandwiches, cake and hot drinks were putting a strain on Norah, who had five children, including twin babies and one under three years old. So we offered to host one of the meetings, and in September 1967, the Bible study moved to 1 Lyndhurst Drive. I turned a bedroom into a lounge so it could be used for counselling or private prayer.

On the first Thursday, nineteen came and two asked Jesus into their lives in that "upper room." In October He blessed me; I was baptised in the Spirit and given the gift of another tongue, with which to praise and worship Him more fully. How He blessed us all!

By January 1968, fifty to sixty young people were coming every Thursday, and we had to have an overflow Bible study group with twenty to twenty-five upstairs! From January to September 1968, numbers never dropped below fifty, and never exceeded sixty! We considered hiring a hall, but the Lord never put His seal on that idea. The numbers had become exhausting, but He dealt with the situation naturally; in September several left for various reasons, such as marriage or university, and the numbers settled to about thirty, and the upstairs room was no longer necessary. At the end of 1968 we decided to swap. In January the Tuesday prayer meeting came to us, and the Thursday Bible study went to Dawson's.

In March 1969, Jean Darnall came and spoke at a meeting at the Public Hall in Harpenden. For several months there had been much prayer. For three Fridays before the meeting, The Group formed a rota and prayed through the night. The Lord blessed it mightily and several people were converted, and others were baptised in the Spirit and received various gifts.

After that, people joined from further afield, St. Albans and Harlow. In April David was baptised in the Spirit and spoke in tongues.

In January this year, 1970, we swapped again; the prayer meeting returned to Dawson's and the study came back to us. The Lord has kept the numbers steady, between twenty and thirty each week, in spite of the normal changes of people leaving the district. He is a wonderful loving, understanding Father and He knows just what we need. However He never allows us to get into a rut! The Holy Spirit keeps us changing and moving on and it is always an adventure - with the Lord. We never know what lies ahead or what new plans He has for us. Praise the Lord!

MARY AUCKLAND

Why I Believe in God

At 16, like most teenagers, I doubted the existence of God. Who does not at some time? Despite my doubts, I continued to go to Church . . . just in case! In September 1967, I found that He does exist. This is the reason why.

Out of curiosity, I went along to a meeting of Christians, where they read the Bible. In these people's faces, I saw something which I knew was not to be found in any human activity or pleasure. I discovered that I too wanted Him. So that night I accepted Jesus into my life as my Saviour, and I realised I was a sinner and asked His forgiveness. I knew then that I had been saved. This is not presumption, for it says in the Bible, "For by grace you have been saved through faith; and this is not your own doing, it is the gift of God."

Surely the question in most people's hearts today is: "Why do we exist?" I have found the purpose of life. It is to live the way God wants me to, and it is a very satisfying way. I have also found happiness, peace and contentment. I have found that being a Christian is not just thinking of God on Sunday in church, but having a personal relationship with the Lord. (Of course, fellowship, as well as prayer and Bible study, is part of a Christian's life.) Jesus guides me and helps me to live my life. He IS the way, the truth and the life.

When you look at the sun, the stars and this earth, and when you consider the babies, who are being born every minute, can you honestly doubt that there is a creator and life-giver? If you can read between the lines of this article, and see the love that I, a young teenage girl, have for the world and for God, can you doubt that He exists and that I have found Him?

If you have not yet found what I have found - God and His son Jesus - take the advice of the Bible: "O taste and see that the Lord is good. Happy is the man who takes his refuge in Him."

VIRGINIA GERAERTS (née Gray) 2011

In 1967 I had just started working at Solleys, the solicitors, when a friend, Jeannette Kineer, told me that there was a free coach trip planned to Earls Court to hear the evangelist Billy Graham, and would I like to go with her? I nearly refused – how glad I am now that I said I would! For many years I had felt the reality of God, but I did not have a spiritual teacher and the Holy Spirit was still a mystery.

At the meeting I was overwhelmed by the sheer number filling the auditorium, the singing and the eagerness of the people. When Billy Graham began to speak I felt that here was a trustworthy man of God. His speech was not passionately enthusiastic. In fact it was quite low key and very logical. He spoke of God with conviction, and backed up his words with verses from the Bible. As his team spread out round the stage, to receive those who would come to the front to 'Give their lives to the Lord,' I deliberately refused to 'give in' to the urge to walk forward and make a commitment. There was such an overwhelming feeling of being in a place of God, I felt like a magnet was pulling me, but I resisted by telling myself I had already given my life to Jesus.

On the coach going home we were all given information about The Harpenden Prayer Group, and I can honestly say that the Billy Graham meeting and The Prayer Group, which I attended subsequently, were two of the most important events in my spiritual life. The meetings seemed to be full of young people, sitting, kneeling or sprawling on the floor. It was true fellowship and a time of growth, especially for those who had made a commitment to Jesus at the Crusade. It was 1967, and at The Group meetings we would pray in tongues, prophesy and worship, very much as the early Christians did.

There was no awareness of differences in denominational worship. We were all together at that time in worship, even though our Sunday worship might be anything from Roman Catholic to URC, Methodist, C.

of E., or none. Now, as I read of the development of worship through the twentieth century and post modernism, I realise that that type of Charismatic worship was very unusual in the 1960's. I believe the Lord was and is doing something unusual in Harpenden. The Methodist Church says that Harpenden is their flagship church in the UK, the young people's Christian organisation, YWAM, have their headquarters at Harpenden Oval, and The Harpenden Group was an early centre of charismatic worship in the 1960's.

In 1969 I moved to Cheshire, got married and had children and grandchildren. Twelve years ago my husband was diagnosed as terminally ill and died. From 1969 to 2000, I always knew God was faithful; He kept his promises to me but I hadn't always kept mine to him. I would pray and come before Him, knowing I was unworthy.

Imagine my surprise, when five years ago I heard in prayer, 'Speak to my people'. I laughed and said to the Lord, 'You must be joking!' He then proceeded to show me a book, and each page, as it was turned, had a different picture from my life on it. They showed scenes bad and good, times of which I was ashamed, times of grief and so on. When the book was closed the voice said, 'That is why I want you to speak to my people.'

For five years I had been asking the Lord to tell me what he wanted me to do, and while I waited I had taken a counselling diploma amongst other things, so that I would be ready. Now I had an answer, but what should I do next? A Licensed Reader at my church suggested I take the Certificate in Ministry course, while exploring where I was being called. This I did. Next, several people (who didn't know each other, including a vicar and my spiritual mentor) told me that all would be made clear at Pentecost. Feeling a tug to go and spend time away from the world, I went to an Anglican Community, the Sisters of Jesus' Way, who run a retreat house. I asked them if they knew why I was there. They invited me to live with them for as long as I liked, as they had received a prophecy and were expecting me! How great is our God. Rather than store my things, I gave most of them away, and moved in with the Sisters at the beginning of the year. There was no TV or radio, chapel every morning at 8am and no conversation after 8pm. My room was tiny with a single wardrobe, and my tasks included cleaning lavatories, but every piece of work was done joyfully for God. It was a wonderful time of growing closer to the Lord - such as times when I would wake at 3 am and have to write in my journal what I had just learned. Amazing!

At Pentecost there were two signs. In chapel I heard a voice say to me (referring to times of despair) 'The times you have not been able to hear me were the times I have been closer to you than I have ever been before.' This was accompanied by a clip from the film Close Encounters of the Third Kind, where the sky is blacked out by a huge UFO hovering over the mountain top! The other was a visitor, who insisted she had to tell me I was not to be a nun, but I was to be a vicar, to speak to the people, and to visit people in hospitals.

So here I am, training in lay ministry as a Licensed Reader in the Church of England. I speak to the people by preaching and leading services and I lead a youth house group. I remember very well my time with The Harpenden Group, and lead the young people in my group in the same format.

I thank God for the time I had with the members of The Group in Harpenden. It was a grounding for my faith and a memory of Christian fellowship, which has never left me through good and bad times.

MARION PUNFORD

I always went to Church, and in December 1965 was confirmed, but it did not mean all I expected it to, and I was disappointed. In the bottom of my heart I thought my religion was not all it should be, yet I did not admit this to myself, and considered myself quite a good Christian. I thought I would progress as a Christian in time, and I suppose I thought of "progress" as getting closer to God. Despite regular church attendance, Bible reading and somewhat forced, laborious prayer, I now realise I had no personal relationship with Jesus Christ, and consequently was very hungry for God. I even talked about Christianity as seen through the Church of England, which I thought was the "Way, the Truth and the Life"! Apart from Roman Catholicism I disliked all other forms of Christianity.

In June 1966, I went forward at the Billy Graham Crusade at Earls Court, in a supposed rededication of my life, but it meant nothing. I was referred to a Bible study group in Harpenden, but did not go as I thought it would be too "evangelical".

One evening, in July 1967, I went along out of curiosity to a "Project" meeting, where the gospel was preached and some witnessed to their faith. I didn't like it very much. Then I met an old school friend, Angela, there, and she was with a group of people from the Bible study group, which I was supposed to have gone to after the Billy Graham Crusade. They said they'd been praying for me since the Crusade and asked me down to The Group. I didn't really want to go, but they offered to take me by car, so, being lazy, I decided to go.

Instead of some kind of Bible lecture by "Bible punching evangelists," I found a group of people with something I hadn't got and very much wanted - a personal relationship with Jesus Christ. After going to The Group three times, on the 29th August, after a prayer meeting which greatly inspired me, I let Jesus come into my life and take over. Then, with this personal relationship with Jesus, I knew I was a real Christian, and everything else, Bible reading, prayer, worship and life itself, seemed to click into place, and the whole of life became a new experience. I love telling others about Jesus and how they can have the great peace and joy which I have found in Him. I thank and praise the Lord for giving me this new and wonderful life, life in this world and Eternal Life. The best way I can describe how I felt when Jesus came into my life, is in the words of a hymn: "Heaven came down, and glory filled my soul!" Hallelujah!

MARK PUNFORD

For ages and ages, I had hungered for that "God thing", that I believed to be real. I was well aware that I needed Him, and every Sunday I went to church and sat at the very back, away from all the others, to try in my own way to be close to God. I did occasionally. This was rare and, as close as I did get, it did not satisfy my hunger. I came out of church more hungry. I used to long to serve God in a much greater way than just going to church. I tried hard to find Him, but in vain. Reason:- I always thought of Him as a "Mysterious God", instead of who He really was: Jesus. I knew I had yet to experience my Creator - Where could I find Him?

Then one day my sister said to me she had met up with a group of people who had "found the way". Immediately she told me the good tidings, and I realised you didn't have to be a vicar to meet God! She showed me references in the New Testament about how to be a Christian. I knew I was on the right track at last, for I saw the "signal box" work in the Bible, but I needed a "station". For weeks Marion grew as a Christian, and as she grew she helped me to grow. I believed it, and soon had the urge to ask not "God up in the sky", but living real Jesus, into my life. I asked for forgiveness for all my sins, and that He would be my Saviour and live with me forever. Then I felt very happy. It was the greatest time of my life and that night Jesus gave me His peace.

As the weeks went by my relationship with Jesus grew till I talked to Him as my friend. Since I have been a Christian, I have benefitted a lot, but above all, Jesus has benefitted, which is of course more important. He now has me as a member of His family. He regularly forgives and inspires me, and keeps me trusting His word day by day. He is my friend. If I lost Him now, I could not live, but I cannot lose Him because we are bound by unbreakable promises. I have found the way. My hunger is satisfied. Jesus is satisfied to have me. I am grateful in the maximum. I no longer think of Him as a far away, non-tangible legend possibility in another world. God, I know, shows Himself in Jesus, for God IS Jesus. Whenever I think of Jesus, I think of a man, all powerful, looking with loving, kind eyes upon the world. Jesus has given me (1) salvation (2) forgiveness of all sins (3) inspiration to believe (4) love to pour out (5) faith (6) guidance (7) everything, though I deserve nothing. I am a true Christian. PRAISE THE LORD!

LYNN LEITH - December 1967

Last year I lived in London. I thought I was a fairly good Christian then, but realise now how far from the truth I was. I went to church, and took an interest in its activities by helping to run a Saturday Link, a kind of Sunday School on Saturday. I suppose I was what you'd call a Christian on Sundays only, and the rest of the week lived for my own pleasure, with no thought of God coming in at all, except for my irregular times of prayer, which never meant much and were never answered. So I really needn't have bothered.

I was nearly always happy, just living for my enjoyment, doing exactly what I wanted to do, soaking up my popularity with other people, and loving every minute of it. However as soon as I got home and was alone, I used to feel terrible, very depressed, very alone, waiting and wondering what I was living for, what anyone was living for and what would happen to us after death. I was genuinely scared of dying. I didn't want to leave all the friends I'd made, and not knowing where I was going made it even worse. It got so bad that I had to go and have a chat to the local curate, but although he helped a bit, he never told me how to get rid of my fear for good.

I was confirmed in November 1964 and was given a new Bible from Mum and Dad, which was read regularly for a few weeks and then began to travel nearer the bookcase every day, and there it stayed until quite recently! I enjoyed Scripture lessons at school, playing the teacher up, drawing maps of Palestine and trying to look interested, while she lectured us on something we didn't understand.

In 1966, I went to the Billy Graham Crusade at Earls Court with a group of people from St. Mary's Church, Wimbledon. During his message, something was telling me that this belief, of his and many others in that place, was also the belief I could easily come to know and believe in very strongly. Although the feeling was very strong that I must go up and receive the Lord Jesus into my heart, I never did. Perhaps the Lord knew that this was not yet my time. He gave me another chance, Praise His name!

In February, we moved from London to Harpenden. I got in contact with two girls I already knew, and they introduced me to Angela, who told me of a Bible study and prayer meeting she attended on Tuesdays and

Thursdays. When she asked me if I would like to go, I shunned her first and second invitation, but decided to go when she asked the third time.

It was Thursday 6th April 1967, when I first went along. When we arrived there were only four other people there, but they seemed different, surprisingly happy, content and at peace with the world, with all its worries and problems that plague one's mind, well mine anyway! We read St. John 15, "I am the true vine." It was amazing to me how many different meanings could be found in just one passage. Afterwards we had coffee, and they told me what joy it brings you to have Jesus Christ in your heart. After we had been talking for some time, I realised that this was for me, that I wanted Jesus in My life. That night at home, I knelt beside my bed, asked the Lord's forgiveness for my past life, and asked Him into my life, to guide me and lead me into doing His will. He came, with all His glory and power, into my life. The next morning, to my surprise, I found that I felt at peace with the world and joyful inside, and I wanted to shout to the world what the Lord can do.

Well, that was 8 months ago now. Since then I have been greatly strengthened and blessed by Him, and know in my heart He is a loving Lord and worthy of all men to be received. He's my friend, my guide and my saviour. Praise God!

JAMES PINDER

I was born into an Anglican Church-going family and tagged along with them until I was fifteen or so, when I started thinking (a rare pastime in those days, as I just followed my nose and "mother nature"!) I soon decided that church-going was a waste of time, as my scientific mind could not grasp the idea of the existence of an invisible, omnipotent God worth worshipping, and at that stage I found the Bible too fantastic. Anyway Jesus did not appear to have much of a place in the church! I was then a fairly staunch anti-Christian and gave, I believe, fairly good opposition to any Christian. I still, at his stage, was forced to attend church regularly at school and occasionally when at home.

The age of eighteen saw me enjoying to the full a London University life, as a "fun-worshipping" youth. However, at the beginning of my final year in London, I was persuaded by a girlfriend to go to a guest service at a city church, which she attended. I had to admit that the atmosphere was very friendly and warm, and for this reason I later returned to this church. I started to go regularly on Sundays for the friendship, and arranged to go with a church party of seventy-six, to Switzerland on a skiing holiday.

It was at Murren in Switzerland, that I realised that these Christians had something that I wanted. All the Christians in the party, many of whom were strangers to me, would always greet me warmly, even if it seemed they should be half asleep and frozen, as at breakfast time! I asked the people questions, and they talked about the saving Blood of Jesus Christ, and finally, on January 6th 1967, I asked Jesus into my life as my personal saviour.

Even though nothing spectacular happened, I did feel comforted and happy to be able to share these other people's warmth. Over the next three weeks or so, I found that I now was warmed by private and communal prayer, and I began to get something out of reading the Word of God, which hitherto had been boring and impersonal; I began to understand things which previously I had not even noticed.

My faith then remained fairly static until I moved to Harpenden, where I sought and found fellowship in late August that year. I believe I was guided! Here I found a group of young people, who had each experienced a similar discovery and acceptance of Jesus. In the discussions, prayer and Bible reading that followed, I began to grow in faith, sometimes jerkily, and sometimes even falling back, but each time to rise again to a peak higher than that attained before the fall - Praise the Lord. I began to understand more fully the perfect work Jesus had done for me, when He became visible as God's sacrificial Lamb, to die for my sins - many of which I never knew I had - and through His great love, to give me a new life till Eternity.

I soon realised that I needed to find Jesus as The Baptiser, to receive strength to witness and preach His gospel. I thank my Lord that on March 22nd 1968, He found me worthy to receive His precious gift of the Holy Spirit, who immediately enriched my prayer with praise and thanksgiving for the Lord.

My one aim now is for a closer walk with God, through Jesus, so that The Spirit can have a free rein in my life. My heart is constantly overflowing with joy and love as I see, one after another, Jesus' promises fulfilled now, just as they were 1950 years ago, in and by His followers. I have proved to myself that "Jesus Christ is the same yesterday, today and forever" To Him be ALL glory. Amen.

VICKY GRANT

On 13th September 1967 I became a Christian. This date also marks the end of a two year search for Christ.

At the age of eleven or twelve I can remember my mother and grandmother telling me of their Spiritualist beliefs. However I was only a child, so everything they said made little impression on me. In 1965, when I was fifteen years old, it was more or less taken for granted that I would start attending the Spiritualist meetings, when the Spiritualists considered me old enough to do so. I discussed this with my friend Marion Punford, who had joined The Group and become a Christian a few weeks before me. She was horrified at the idea and told me many times not to become a Spiritualist. My mother told me not to take any notice of Marion, because she knew very little about Spiritualism. Praise the Lord, I did take notice of Marion's advice and did not become a Spiritualist.

During that time I was very depressed because I did not know what was the right thing to do - whether or not to go to the Spiritualist meetings. I was very confused and I was beginning to doubt the existence of God. After much thought, I decided that the best thing to do would be to commit suicide. This, I thought, would enable me to discover whether or not God existed. If He did not exist, death would be like a deep sleep, and if He did, nothing could possibly harm me.

At the age of sixteen, I left school and went to college. Marion and I lost touch with each other until several months later, when I met a Christian from the Church of England, who asked Ken David, the curate of St. Nicholas', to visit me. A few weeks later he came, and it was arranged that I would go to church with Marion on Sunday mornings. I attended regularly for almost a year, but still could not find the Lord. Therefore, as I did not know Him, it was difficult to love Him.

In early September 1967 during the summer holidays, I was staying with Marion, and of course, she witnessed to me. I went to a prayer meeting, and for the first time I felt the Lord's presence. I thought for a short time and almost decided that I did not want the Lord in my life. Then I asked myself, "Do you want the Lord in your life or not?" The first answer was, "No", and the second was, "Yes."

PETER GOULD

....."I've got so much to do since I became a Christian." There are many young people in our Group, and we usually see each other on a Friday or Saturday evening as well - you know, we "congregate" round somebody's house or something. Yes, homes really are much better now I am a Christian. Friendships are on a completely different level than those between non-Christians; they are deeper and more sincere, if you see what I mean.

Now I must get down to the point, for what I have just said is also true with a relationship between a Christian boy and a Christian girl. Their association is very different from that of a non-Christian boy and girl, and much more rewarding and satisfying because of this. They think of and do different things. The point I'm trying to make, is that I've now got a completely different outlook on life, especially where a boy and a girl are concerned - a new "moral outlook" you might say.

I no longer believe in sex before marriage. Does that shock you? I feel it is unnecessary; one of the partners is always hurt, it gives purely temporary satisfaction and it usually leads to disillusionment in the end. To me this is not worth risking. Before, I used to enjoy going to bed with a girl. It got to such a stage that if I wasn't "getting it", I'd sulk and turn moody. I did believe in sex before marriage, quite sincerely really, and I honestly thought there was nothing wrong in it. I would gladly have advocated a society of free love. Oh I praise the Lord that He rescued me in time from all those things, those mistaken values, those depravities.

It makes me so sad to see others going the same way, the same way from which I was rescued, and they are going that way, there is no denying it. If you look at it honestly and objectively, the whole, or at least a great part, of my generation are immoral, or would be if they got half the chance. Can any one of them say they are really happy and content and really feel secure? No, not one, not one! One party is always hurt in the end, and they both finish up with nothing - they are alone and unhappy. Oh, there is so much evil in young people nowadays - they are in the grip of Satan without knowing it.

The trouble is, you see, these people, and I was the same, never stop to think or consider the harm they are doing to themselves and to others. To them sex is everything. If only they knew that sex is not everything. Oh, if only they would stop and think, before it is too late. If only the whole world would stop and think before it is too late. You know, I used to think I couldn't do without sex, but now I know I can. This is because I've put my trust in Jesus and He, praise His name, has delivered me from these "sins of the flesh". I thank Him for it, because I could never have done this by myself. He promises you freedom from all that is wrong and evil, and if you have faith in Him, He keeps those promises. Jesus never lets you down. People do. Dear Lord, how I wish others, who are like I was, would do the same - put their trust in you. They would be much happier for it. Dear Lord, give me strength to tell them how they may escape from those invisible chains, which get tighter every day.

Well, now you've read for yourself how much I have changed. Now I believe the Lord will provide me with a girl, a girl with whom it is not necessary to have sexual relations, because we'll both be tuned in to different wavelengths than the average boy and girl. We'll have something more, something which is very much spiritual, something which leaves no time for sex and bed. We will be much happier and healthier for it.

Now I don't go out with any girl, as that would be just tempting myself unnecessarily. For me to leave it at that would be nonsensical. You see, the point is, I wouldn't want to go out with just any girl. As I am a Christian I could only go out with a Christian girl, a girl who thinks and worships the same as I do, a girl who has given her life to Christ. Any relationship without Christ is fruitless and pointless, and I don't desire that kind of relationship. Why should I, when I know there is something far better just round the corner, or should I say somebody? And that somebody is worth waiting for, because she has been chosen for me by Jesus and we'll both know it, believe you me. Now, I ask you, why should I spoil this by flitting around from girl to girl, bed to bed? It's just not worth it, when you've got Jesus to choose you a partner. Human beings can make mistakes, but He can't. Praise Him!

I not only believe God exists, I know He exists, for only He could have picked me up out of the depths of despair and given me new life, a life which is worth living. Truly, I can say that in Christ Jesus I was "born again".

PETER GOULD

Why I Believe in God

Although I believed in God He was never real to me. He did not affect the things I said or did. The kind of life I was living, before I came to have a deeper awareness of Him, was one which I knew He would have disapproved of.

The story of how I came to have this deeper and more personal relationship with Him begins in July 1967, when I went to a meeting in St. Albans, for it was there that I first heard the full gospel of Jesus Christ. The speaker said that Jesus Christ could satisfy every need, fill the empty gap in my heart, and I certainly had one such gap in my heart, a result of just having lost the only girl I had ever loved. Could Jesus take her place? Well, I had nothing to lose and so, largely out of interest, I stepped forward.

It was as a result of this, that I came into contact with a group of Christians in Harpenden and I began to go to their meetings, where I learnt more of God and Christ. Soon I thought I was a Christian, for, as well as enjoying their Bible Readings, I found myself agreeing with their Christian principles.

How mistaken I was! I soon found that I could still do things I had done previously, which I should then have considered unchristian, and therefore should not have done. However, God's word had bitten too far into my heart for me to ignore it, and the next time I tried reverting to my old ways, I realised it was impossible - God and sin were incompatible - and a "vision" I had, showed me the necessity of making a choice between God and myself. I saw two roads, one narrow, the Christian road, and the other wide, the easy road of worldly pleasures.

I had taken a middle course, which did not work, and my troubles had soon come pouring back. There was only one thing to do, to ask God's forgiveness and accept Jesus Christ as my personal Saviour. The moment I did this and brought myself to the foot of that Cross at Calvary, the burden of my sins and problems felt lighter. My prayer had been heard.

In 2 Corinthians Paul says, "If any man be in Christ he is a new creature; old things are passed away, behold all things become new". This certainly applied to me. My outlook on life has been completely changed, and I no longer do the things I used to do, not because I must not, but because I do not want to.

Jesus once said that He came so we might have life and have it more abundantly. How this is true. Now I am really living, for I am walking in fellowship with God and His Son. I have eternal joy in my heart. Jesus has certainly kept His promise and I praise Him for it.

I not only "believe" God exists; I know He exists, for only He could have picked me up out of the depths of despair and given me new life, a life which is worth living. Truly can I say that in Christ Jesus I was "born again".

NICOLA BARCLAY-WATT

"But have you put your trust in Jesus Christ?" asked my sister, to find out if I was a Christian. I did not realise it then, but this was the beginning of the turning upside-down of my life, though at the time I just thought she was being "super holy." After all, didn't I go to church, say my prayers and read my Bible? I had been baptised and confirmed. I was pretty sure that if I continued going to church, etc., and living a decent enough life, I would get to Heaven in the end.

However her words must have struck home in some way. Sadly, as I see it now, I became more religious and read my Bible twice a day. (There's nothing wrong with this normally I know, but I was trying to earn my way to Heaven) I knew that Sara and her fiance understood their faith, lived their faith each day, and were given peace and joy from their faith. What had I from my faith? Nothing!

It was all a ritual, but I was too proud to go and ask them how I could get this joy out of life too.

When I went to London, Sara took me along to a Christian club. I could see that the people there had this joy that I was seeking too, but I thought it was rather unnecessary to go round talking about God all the time. A few weeks later at this club, they had a speaker who took the verse, "If anyone thirst let him come unto me and drink" (John 7:37). I knew that I was "thirsting" and wanted Jesus in my life. At the end of the meeting there was an invitation, for those who wanted to ask Jesus into their lives to go forward. I went forward and was spoken to personally by a girl, who afterwards said a prayer with me. I knew then that my life was opening up in an exciting new dimension. That night I went home walking on air! I read my Bible and discovered that it lived. God really had come to Earth to reveal Himself to man. Not only that, but He reveals Himself to man today if people will hand their lives over to Jesus Christ.

PAT THOMLINSON (née Hogan) - 21st October 2009

When I look back on "The Group" I think I have to start at the very beginning of my conversion, from a static Christian to having a real relationship with my Lord! The Lord took me in hand so gently and kindly, leading me on in those early days, ensuring I had all the help, support and fellowship essential to a newborn babe in the faith.

After much soul searching, at the tender age of twenty, and only six months married, I sat on the edge of my bed, dusted down my Bible and opened the pages, asking God to become real to me. Immediately I felt His love encompass me, and had that incredible feeling of peace fill me to capacity.

Still in wonder of what was happening to me, that afternoon I went for an interview for a job at the Bank in St Albans. As I entered the Bank Manager's office, my eyes were drawn to a print of a famous painting of Jesus. "The Lord turned and looked upon Peter and Peter remembered." Underneath the picture in large print were the words, "IS IT NOTHING TO YOU?" I must have looked at this picture for a long minute, because very gently the manager said, "Well - is it?"

I shook myself and looked at him in wonder and said slowly, *"It's just become everything to me!"* For a horrid minute I thought, *"What am I saying?"* but his face broke into a smile and he just said, *"That's great!"* I remember nothing else about the interview, except that I got the job!

Going home on the top of the bus I was on cloud nine, but the surprises didn't stop there! On the seat in front of me were two girls I had known from school, Virginia Gray and Carole Windsor. They turned to greet me, and Virginia said *"What's happened to you? You're like the cat that's got the cream!"* Without thinking, I told them *"I've just got a job in the bank and I've become a committed Christian."* For the second time that day I inwardly recoiled and wondered what on earth I was saying! Before I could even flush with embarrassment, their faces lit up and they enthusiastically told me that they were Christians and went to a lovely Bible Study Group in Harpenden, and would I like to come?

That was the start of an incredible journey and a most amazing experience. When I arrived at The Group at Lyndhurst Drive, the home of Alma and David Pinkney, I was made really welcome The large room was full of people of all ages, maybe fifteen or so, all sitting round on chairs, cushions and some even on the floor. All had Bibles in their hands - something I'd never seen before, even in church! Somebody opened the meeting in prayer - spontaneous prayer from the heart not from a book - wow! Then Bibles were opened, a few verses read and discussion began As the talk progressed, the words we had read came alive and I realised that this was a Living Truth, relevant not just to this day and age, but to me! I hung on to every word like the thirsty woman at the well, drinking everything in. A young man called Bill Kemp talked with great enthusiasm and excitement, of things that had happened to him and what the Lord had shown him, and finished off by enthusing, *"Oh He's marvellous and I love Him!"* It was so uplifting and definitely contagious! There was so much to take in and learn and the meeting flew by. At last there was a time of prayer, and it was the most special time I had ever experienced. Although I went to many Bible studies and prayer meetings after that, this first one will remain in my memory for ever.

The prayers were heartfelt, natural and spontaneous, just people talking to their Lord. A small silence was broken as someone started to sing, and everyone gradually joined in. The words hit home like a hammer blow and it's always been a favourite of mine, though that night it was new to me.

Reach out and touch the Lord as He passes by
You'll find He's not too busy to hear your heart cry
He's passing by this moment your needs to supply
Reach out and touch the Lord as He passes by.

I closed my eyes and held out my hands and knew that the Lord was there walking among us and blessing us, just like He did in the upper room.

After that there was no turning back and I went regularly to the Bible study and to the prayer meetings. Dawson and Norah gently led me on in the faith. Their strength and love were straight from the heart of God, as they opened up their home for His work.

At the meetings there was always a coffee time afterwards, and this is the only group I have ever attended, before or since, when the chat over coffee was still about the Lord! Never did I hear secular chat, like Mr. So-and-So has a new car, or the weather or politics. People loved the Lord so much that they couldn't stop talking about Him, and often discussion held at the meeting would carry on in small groups.

Norah is a darling and has a great down to earth sense of humour. At one prayer meeting some lovely West Indian Christians (Augustine and Beryl) from Luton were invited over, and they were wonderful! Enthusiastic and voluble, they soon were "Praising de Lord" in loud voices – over and over again. Being unused to this yet, and suffering from an acute fit of the giggles, I quietly left the room and went to the kitchen to put the kettle on. There, to my surprise, was Norah with another lady in fits of laughter, and we all hugged each other and wept with laughing. *"It's the neighbours!"* gasped Norah when she could speak. *"What must they be thinking?"*

Sometimes the prayer meetings were very deep, with long silences or only quiet murmurings, and at other times there was singing with a lot of verbal prayer and people speaking in tongues – this was something I'd heard of but never really understood!

My Bible became my favourite book – so much so that I took it to work so I could carry on reading in my lunch hour, underlining passages and marking the margin. The Bank Manager was super and helped me with many answers to my questions. After eating my lunch, I would often go down to the Abbey and sit in the prayer chapel. This "gift of tongues" was so intriguing, that one day in the chapel I asked the Lord if He would give it to me. How confident we are when we're young!

Later that week, only a few days before my twenty-first birthday, I went to a prayer meeting at Dawson's. I always felt more comfortable kneeling in front of my chair with my head in my arms on the seat of the chair, and as I knelt that night, I had the most overwhelming conviction of my sin. It was awful! I felt that I had put Jesus on the cross, thrust the crown of thorns on His poor head, and the weight of my sin was intolerable! How could I even think of being given the gift of His Holy Spirit? Kneeling down with my head bowed, the tears streamed silently down my cheeks. Then a kindly arm was laid on my shoulders, and hands rested on my head. Dawson had known of my distress, in the amazing way he always knew if someone was in need. I couldn't even gasp out what I was feeling, but I didn't need to! *"You're forgiven,"* said Dawson softly *"It's all washed away – you're clean and new and you can start praising the Lord."*

He laid hands on me again, and although my tears still fell, they were now tears of joy, as I felt so much love and praise and joy welling up from right inside. He'd forgiven all that sin; the burden was gone and I was clean. Over and over I thanked Him, and then found that words weren't enough, and I overflowed with the Spirit in a tongue of incredible beauty and fluency.

So you see, God, Dawson and The Group have been the largest influence on my life, apart from Mum and Dad. Yes, I've had dry times, sad experiences and even doubts, but when I remember The Group and the love, the fellowship and incredible witnesses of the people there, all sadness and doubts dissolve as I give thanks for the way the Lord has had control over my life in every detail.

MARTIN HOGAN 1969 - updated 2009

It all began for me with my sister Pat's twenty first birthday party. We were all invited to the Plumber's Loft for an evening party. I didn't have a girlfriend at the time. However there was a girl at work, who was very keen on me, so I asked her to accompany me to the party, and she accepted the invitation without hesitation! As parties go, it was OK. No alcohol, and everyone seemed to be a religious freak. Pat had started to attend the weekly Bible Study and Prayer Group, which was simply called The Group!

I took very little notice of this, being a good Anglican server, and being deeply involved with my church, I didn't feel the need to go to yet more meetings. However, during the evening my partner and I were deliberately separated. While one person had a go at converting her, another, a girl called Marion Punford, had a go at me. Her opening gambit was "Are *you saved?*" After suffering for about half-an-hour, I excused myself, rescued my partner, and without excusing ourselves left the party and went for a drive. I was so embarrassed for her. She was just grateful that I rescued her. We had a pleasant evening together. As we had missed most of the party food I took her for a meal and then went home. It wasn't until the next day at work that I realised just how keen on me she was. Various people said to me, "I hear you had a great evening last night, nudge nudge, wink wink!"

Knowing there was a nice young man who worked for me, who really fancied her, I spoke to her, and said, "Thank you for coming with me", and then, as gently as I could, told her that I didn't feel there was any future in our relationship and that Tim was very keen to ask her out. They soon got together and continued as a couple for some years.

At the same time another sister, Virginia, got involved with another group of Christians at Loughborough, where she was at Library College. She came home for the Summer, and one evening I came home from work to find my youngest sister, Felicity, very agitated and upset. I couldn't get her to tell me what was wrong at first, but wrongly blamed Virginia and we had a row. I left the house fuming and went for a walk. After walking for ages, I found myself in the middle of the field of corn, sitting under a tree. It had once been two fields but most of the hedge had been removed except for a clump of ancient trees, making it one big field.

I sat on the ground and leaned against the tree. I cried out to God, "What's happening to the family? We were all Christians, and everything was fine until Pat and Ginny got involved with religious sects. Please God, help us. Sort this out and bring them back into the fold." Quick as a flash the answer came back, "Don't worry about Pat or Virginia; it's you I want." I didn't know what to make of that! I had always been a Christian. I was the one who went to church twice every Sunday, and I was on the PCC!

For some weeks after that encounter, the phrase, "*It's you I want,*" niggled me. I felt I needed a Bible Study or something. The trouble was, our church didn't do Bible Studies! The only one I had ever come across was The Group, so I resolved to go.

After finding out where and when they met, I set out, armed with the only Bible I had, a James Moffett translation, which my mother's aunt had given me when I was 12. I walked up and down the street several times, and watched loads of people arrive at the house. Several times I stood at a bus-stop on the corner, pretending to wait for a bus, because I was too shy and embarrassed to go in! Eventually I plucked up the courage and at 7:30 on the dot, I knocked on the door. It was opened wide. Nearly as wide was the welcoming smile on the face of the beautiful young lady who opened it. "*Come in if you're beautiful*", she said! Of course this threw me completely. I stammered, "*Is this where the Bible study is held please?*"

Now it was her turn to look embarrassed, *"Oh, sorry, yes you must be new, come on in and I'll introduce you."*

As the door closed behind me I caught sight of a withered, wrinkled, but smiling face that had appeared around the corner. It was our hostess, Alma Pinkney. Immediately she took over and asked my name. When I told her she said, "Oh, you must be Pat's brother. Come in, come in," and I was 'in'. I was shown to a seat. All the chairs in the large sitting room were around the edge of the room, and as I sat down I saw they were all occupied, except one. Seated on the floor were about thirty young people, all with Bibles open and sheets of paper, which I later learned were the words of the endless choruses we sang before the Bible study started, accompanied on a guitar. I knew none of the songs because choruses were not a part of our church culture at this time. However I soon found I really liked the lively music, and the sentiments of so many of them, which were of course based on scripture. Some even prompted me to look up the Bible references they were taken from.

The study that evening was from the Gospel according to St Mark. The group had just started studying it, and would be working through it over the following weeks. It was led by an Anglican lay reader called Dawson Price. I could cope with lay readers; they were a part of the world I knew. His leadership style was interesting. There was no doubt he was the leader, yet everyone was able to chip in and make comments and observations. There was much page-turning, as individuals looked up cross references and commented on them. That evening we only covered a few verses, but I was amazed what gems came out.

Several things struck me about the evening. We all felt valued, which engendered a sense of worth. No matter how small or trivial the comments, they were treated with the same thoughtful consideration and encouragement. Everyone was enthusiastic about God and Jesus, and really believed the Bible was the Word of God. The comments were prayerful, and every issue raised was handled sensitively.

We finished with about twenty minutes of open prayer, during which many bared their souls in an honest and transparent way, that I had not encountered before outside of the family. I felt truly at home. After the meeting I was able to meet and talk to some of The Group and enjoy a mug of hot chocolate, with what I came to discover was the special treat our hosts David and Alma always gave us, "Jaffa Cakes".

I had learned, or rather gleaned, that as well as the weekly Bible Study, there was a weekly Prayer Meeting. Finding out where and when it took place however, was not easy; it seemed like a closely guarded secret. Eventually I found out that it was held at the home of Dawson and Norah Price, every Tuesday evening. I received many comments like, "Are you sure you're really ready for a Prayer Meeting yet?" These comments only firmed my resolve to go.

Tuesday took forever to come, but when it did I set off, and arrived half an hour before the meeting was due to start. This was a good opportunity to talk to Dawson and Norah, our hosts. From Dawson I learned that they had prayed for me every day since Thursday. I also learnt a little about how The Group started.

Soon people began arriving for the prayer meeting, and again I was surprised how many people there were. The house was smaller than the one used for the Bible study, but still there were about thirty of us. It was a fine autumn evening. So for the first half-hour the setting sun streamed in the windows, filling the room with light. We sang some choruses, accompanied by a single guitarist, and then turned to prayer. As we began to pray the daylight dimmed, and the room became quite dark. No-one seemed to notice, and no-one turned on any lights. Many people prayed, and many of the prayers seemed unconnected, but it didn't seem to matter. For some time I prayed with eyes closed, just soaking in the atmosphere and the amazing sense of fellowship that was almost tangible. After two hours the prayer time ended, and refreshments were served. Eventually we all went home.

For nearly fifteen years I hardly missed a Bible study or prayer meeting, soaking up the teaching and sometimes making contributions. I met some amazing people and was part of a fantastic work of God, which was so right for that time and that place.

The second time I attended the prayer meeting is worthy of a mention. The meeting began as usual, with songs of praise, but we were soon down to prayer. I was kneeling on the floor in front of my chair, facing the wall with my eyes firmly shut, and deep in prayer. The vocal prayers of those around washed over me like a tide washing the beach. After some time I heard a voice clearly speak in my ear. It was as clear as if someone had spoken to me, and I knew that it was God. "Martin turn around and open your eyes." What followed needs a little history to fully understand.

The story really began when I was twelve years old, and had just started attending Townsend Secondary Modern School for Boys in St. Albans. Our headmaster was a deeply committed Christian called Mr Twigg. Although we never dared call our teachers by their Christian names we made it a sort of duty to learn their first names, and George was Mr Twigg's first name. It was the first one I ever discovered. George took us for R.E. and he was an interesting and knowledgeable teacher. In those days, R.E. meant Christianity. We did learn about other faiths, but they came under a special module called Comparative Religion.

In my first year with George we looked at the Early Church, and used as our reference point The Acts of the Apostles. I was fascinated, and, I might say, somewhat confused. I had always been brought up to believe that the Church of England had 'got it right'. What I saw, in the ritual and practice of the church I attended, bore no resemblance to what I read about in The Book of Acts! When I asked George about it, he referred me to the Church's practice of breaking bread together and the rite of Holy Communion. However, I wasn't satisfied.

One night I prayed, asking God to show me what the 'real church' was like. I fell asleep, and in my sleep I had a vision, or dream. It was this: I was in a room full of people. They were all people I knew, and yet, at that time, I didn't know any of them! They were all in an attitude of prayer, some sitting, some lying, some standing and some kneeling. They all had a look of peace on their faces, and I just knew that they all knew the Lord Jesus Christ personally. Although I remembered the vision in the morning, I thought very little about it. I just had the assurance I needed, that the real church still existed. All I had to do was to find it.

On the occasion of my second prayer meeting, I heard the words "Martin, turn around and open your eyes." The Vision or dream of eleven years before was not in my mind at all, but as I obeyed, sat back in my chair and opened my eyes, the vision or dream and the reality of the moment, overlapped and became one! I knew I had at last found what I was searching for; I had found the church and I had truly come home! The Group became my spiritual home for many years, and the bonds of friendship and love built up in that fellowship have stayed with me all my life. People at the church I was attending unfortunately didn't understand my need and all that The Group stood for. I suffered a lot of verbal abuse from the very people who should have been supportive and happy for me. My family, however, was thrilled, and supported me all the way. Mum and Dad attended The Group on and off for a number of years, which was very special for me.

LORNA HOGAN (née Wood)

I feel enormously blessed by being part of The Group as a young adult, from 1969 until 1983.

Over the years, The Group has always been a yardstick to me of what Church should be: an informal meeting in the home, where we prayed and studied together, with an emphasis on listening prayer. What did the Lord want us to pray and say and do? We ate together and shared. There was a lot of laughter. It was never dull. The Group was better than any church service I have ever been to.

In The Group respect and kindness were shown to people of all ages and walks of life, including a muddled middle-aged lady, broken by her divorce, a lonely pensioner, who had never read a book, a local GP, a Cockney lady full of questions, a company director, lively teenagers, troubled teenagers, a girl with Downs Syndrome, a teacher, the young and the old, people with plenty of money and education, and people with little. Such differences were irrelevant. It was like family. There was no snobbery and no gossip.

In spite of the pressure Dawson was under at his responsible job in London, and their demanding family of five young children, Dawson and Norah were always available and good natured, and pleased to see people, and were never phased by people's troubles and needs.

We experienced many answers to prayer during those years. I met Martin at The Group, and by March 1971, we had been engaged nearly a year. We felt we should remain in Harpenden, but could not afford any of the available properties for sale. Suddenly, Martin felt led to set a date to get married in six weeks time! Within six days he saw a terraced cottage advertised in the paper for private sale, in Coldharbour Lane, for £5250 (still a considerable sum in those days!) which we could just afford, and our offer was accepted! A couple in The Group gave us a cheque for £780, a most generous gift, but rather an odd amount! In the end, after the solicitor had been paid, it was exactly the amount we were short of! We loved that cottage: it was on the edge of the countryside and had an extension on the back, which made a super workshop for Martin. We were able to host lots of meetings there.

I had been quite depressed for several years, and used to cry all day on Saturdays. Poor Martin! In September 1972, we went for a week, to the Whatcombe House Community in Dorset, which David and Alma had joined. One day the warden, Reg East, prayed for me. It became apparent I needed healing of memories from a break-up with a previous boyfriend. The bleak depression immediately disappeared and has never came back in over thirty-eight years!

In 1978 during a prayer meeting in our cottage, our daughter Maria was crying. She was only two, and suffering from a third recurrence of a painful bladder infection. Two courses of antibiotics had not worked. People prayed for her, and she was healed that same night, and the infection never came back!

We had very little money, and the Lord provided many things we needed, many quite mundane. For example, I prayed for a bookcase for the children, and two days later, Martin's sister, Ginny, said she had a bookcase she wanted to get rid of. Was I interested? Once we found a box of food on the doorstep. We had told no one of our need.

DAVID WESTON - 1969

In August 1966 I lost a lot of sight, and when I went to the hospital they decided to start me on tablets for glaucoma. After a few months the trouble got worse and I was given drops as well as tablets. By Christmas that year, I was taking drops four times a day and tablets morning and night. I was extremely short-sighted and could only see a few inches clearly in front of me. Then it was decided I was to have an operation. I went in for it at the end of January 1967. At Easter I lost my sight completely.

Just after Easter I went back to work. I was in a state of 'non-existence'. This state continued for about three weeks, after which depression started. They were only minor attacks at first, but gradually built up to extreme depression, and the pain started again in my eyes.

When I went to the hospital one Thursday, the drops and tablets were recommenced. I was in a state of deep despair. In June I went on holiday, after which I felt much better. I still continued with the tablets and drops until I had another operation in August, which was a complete failure. Instead of reducing the pain, it increased tremendously. I had pain all down my face too. Three weeks after the operation I was again in a state of utter despair. Just after this I had an alcohol injection to take away the pain. This was successful for about five weeks.

On Tuesday the fourteenth of November 1967, Lynn Leith came to see me (I met her in the pet shop) She asked me if I would like to go the next day to a full gospel meeting at Welwyn Pentecostal Church, and I decided to go. I went forward for healing, and at the end of the service I asked the Lord into my life. I went away not feeling much different. A week later, at a Tuesday night prayer meeting, I felt a terrific, overwhelming presence of the Lord for the first time. On Wednesday morning I realised that for one week the Lord had been in my life. Praise the Lord! After a time, I felt an amazing love inside me for God. This love grew up to a point where it overflowed to the people near me. This love has given me a deeper understanding, a meaning and a purpose in life.

I know that one day the Lord will heal me so that I can see, but although I have not got physical sight, I can see God, and that is the most important thing to me. Praise the Lord! Glory Hallelujah! Thank you for reading this, because it has come from my heart. Praise the Lord!'

VIRGINIA WESTON (née Hogan) 2011

Memories of The Group, (*and of Dawson & Norah Price*)

I was converted at college in 1965, and first met Dawson and Norah when I came home the following Easter and went to a prayer meeting at the house of a lady called Gwen. This was pre-Group days, and it was just a brief passing of ships in the night, for Gwen and I went to the Evangelical Church, whereas Dawson and Norah went to the Anglican Church. Being away in Loughborough, and then working and living away from home for three years after graduation, I only heard occasional reports about them and the Prayer and Bible Study Group they had started. Both my brother and sister, who by then were Christians, were members of The Group. I had little idea then what a big part the Prices were to play in my life.

In the summer of 1970 I came back to live in Harpenden, and stayed with my aunt and grandmother, to alleviate space at home. But one afternoon, while visiting my parents, my brother Martin came home from work and invited me to The Group meeting that evening. Neither he nor I realised that the invitation was to change the course of my life!

I went gladly, and thoroughly enjoyed it. The meeting was held at the Pinkneys' house, and it was packed with enthusiastic and erudite young people! I sat next to a young man called David, who was blind and had his guide dog with him. We got talking and it turned out that he lived very near to my aunt. We started doing things together on Saturdays, and four weeks after first meeting, we got engaged! He was twenty eight and I was twenty six, so there seemed little point in a long engagement. We got married in June, five weeks after Martin and Lorna's wedding.

Dawson and Norah were always there in the background in those early days of marriage and parenthood. They kept open house, and Norah's greeting of delight when she opened the door to you, let you know that it was never inconvenient or a bad moment, but that you were truly welcome.

Her parenting was a joy to learn from. I remember her laughter when recounting how her little twins had fed Trisha's dog Jacob a whole packet of cornflakes and a pint of milk, because they thought he looked hungry! One day, while I was chatting to her in the kitchen, one of the twins came in crying because the other two small fry wouldn't let him play with them. She dried his tears and took him on her lap and said, "Never mind love, what would **you** like to do?" He thought for a moment and then said, "I'd like to go fishing!" There was no way Norah could take him fishing, with other children in the garden and a guest in the kitchen, but she responded instantly. "Okay! Let's go fishing!" She sat him on the edge of the table, put a bucket of water on the floor below him, improvised a rod with a cane, string and a bent pin, and we cut out a few paper fishes which we floated on top of the water. He spent a happy half-hour, trying to catch the soggy little bits of paper, and then rejoined his brothers, who by then had forgotten that they weren't playing with him!

I tell this little story because it illustrates Dawson and Norah's approach to parenting in The Group! They never dictated, or pontificated, but were always in the background, encouraging, accepting, and respecting everyone, and listening to their opinion. Some of us were pretty raw and wet behind the ears, and, thinking back, I wonder if some of the things they heard from us, with regard to our theological ideas, ever made their hair stand on end! But they never corrected! Dawson would suggest, or bring us to another scripture, but **always** he listened courteously to our green ideas, as we sat around the word of God, animatedly discussing it.

It was the same with his authority. It was never pushed, never even seemed to be exerted! Yet his gentle hand was there in the background, to lift us up when we stumbled, and pat us in the back when we did well. The Group led the little Sunday service in the hospital once a month, and the jobs of speaking, leading and praying at it, were always brought to the prayer meeting the week before, for everyone to pray over. Dawson never appointed who was to do anything. He left it to the Holy Spirit to tell us, and he expected that, however new a baby we were in the Lord, the Spirit would speak to us. It was an amazing time of growing in the Lord, as the Holy Spirit did speak to us, did lay the jobs on people's hearts to do, or confirm who was to do them. It all stemmed from the fact that Dawson truly did see the Holy Spirit as being the leader, and had implicit faith that He **would** lead us, **would** speak to us!

We saw many miracles in those days, as people were healed or given guidance, or those unsaved friends we prayed for came to the Lord. I can truly say it was a time of revival.

In 1980 David and I moved to St Albans, and being without our own transport, were not able to attend any more meetings of The Group, except on rare occasions. Yet Dawson and Norah's influence, and the example of their lives, lived out before us in openness and love, has never left us. It has been the plumb line in our lives and unconsciously we find ourselves evaluating all other experiences against it.

"But the wisdom that is from above is first pure, then peaceable, gentle, and easy to be entreated, full of mercy and good fruits, without partiality, and without hypocrisy." James 3:17

Dawson worked for the Atomic Energy Authority, and he was truly a man who treated everyone alike. They lived simply, in a semi-detached house on the new estate behind the cemetery. As he saw to all the bills, Norah never knew what his salary was or understood what his exact job was. He gave her the housekeeping she needed, and because she was a very thrifty Yorkshire woman, she was a splendid housekeeper. If anything untoward was needed, Dawson would carefully think about it and evaluate if they really needed it and whether they could afford it, and she relied entirely on his measured judgements to keep them all on track.

She would often phone his office in a crisis, and speak to his very nice secretary. The conversations would run something like this:

"Hallo, it's Norah Price here. Can I speak to Dawson a moment?"

"Hallo Mrs Price, how are you? I'm afraid he's in a meeting at the moment. Can I give him a message or do you want him to call you back?"

"Well can you just ask him to pray for Jim (*or whoever was the latest victim of disaster!*) He's broken his leg (*or arm, or put his head through a plate glass door! The boys usually did things thoroughly!*)

"Of course. I'll give him the message, just as soon as he is free."

Very occasionally Dawson would ring Norah from the office and say, "We have a visitor from (somewhere overseas) and the meeting he has come over for isn't until Monday. He'll be stuck in the hotel for the weekend. Can I bring him home to stay?"

"Of course," would be the answer, and Jim (who was the oldest) would be turned out of his bedroom and bedded down somewhere else, to make way for the visitor. Norah's cooking was good sustaining Yorkshire fare, and plenty of it, with five hungry children to satisfy, and the guest, whose English could be variable, would be welcomed into the normal vivacious family life of the Prices, and fed well.

One day Dawson told Norah that there was to be a twenty-fifth anniversary dinner of the AEA, and that she was to come to it with him, and to buy a new dress for it. She was taken aback! That was his world and she had never had anything to do with it before! Posh Dos were not her thing, but he wouldn't let her argue, and insisted she buy a really nice outfit. (I can't remember if the outfit included a hat as well – I suspect it did) He told her which train to catch to London and promised her that someone would meet her at the station and bring her to his office, so they could go together.

She dutifully sailed up to London in her new outfit, and was met – by a chauffeur with a magnificent limo, who treated her as if she was royalty! She was driven to the AEA building, where she was taken, not to some little office with a nice homely secretary, as she had always imagined, but up in the lift, until eventually they came to a sort of penthouse suit of offices, with a magnificent reception area and the elegant receptionist, whose friendly voice was the only thing she recognised! She was given a beautiful welcome by this woman, whom she had spoken to so many times over the years, and ushered into Dawson's "Office"

"Ginny!" she said as she recounted the experience to me, "It was massive. It covered the whole of the rest of that floor!" She described it in an awed voice. There was an area with lovely plush sofas and a coffee table, and another area that had a huge conference table with chairs round it. His desk was a gigantic polished affair set in lonely splendour at the end of the room, and along one wall were very discreet cupboards. One had a large hanging space for spare suits and stuff like that, and one opened out into a sort of en suite, with somewhere to wash and brush up if he was going to an evening meeting!

When Dawson came in, she remonstrated with him. "Why did you never tell me you were so important? All those times I rang your secretary when I wanted you to pray! And what about those people you've brought to stay? I'll bet they were really important! Why didn't you tell me?"

Dawson couldn't understand why she was so upset. "But they all enjoyed coming, love. You know they did. They were always very appreciative of your hospitality!"

And he really **didn't** see why she was so upset with him. Dawson was always the same to all people. Every person had intrinsic worth, and position and title, or lack of it, were alike irrelevant to him. He saw each person as a valued soul in the sight of God, and treated him or her with the same courtesy and kindness, and viewed himself with humility – if he viewed himself at all! For he was not a person who thought of himself overmuch; it was always the other person he was thinking of. This story is a long one, but it illustrates so well his lack of partiality in his dealings with people. The youngest and lowliest in that great building would have received the same courtesy from him as did the Directors. I suppose that is why God had great pleasure in allowing him to be promoted later to that very same level!

In 1992 David and I moved back to Harpenden. By then our children had grown up and left home. We began to attend Dawson and Norah's meetings again. Like all things that are organic, it has changed over the years we have known it. The young singles that had attended in the early years, some of who were still at school, had all finished their education, got married and moved on. But it was now over twenty years since its beginnings, and Dawson and Norah themselves were older. Their children too had flown the nest. The people the Lord was now bringing to them to nurture were older. There were fewer of them, but the core of The Group was made up of solid, praying Christians, with others drawn in as the Lord willed. The Group was now a combined Bible study/prayer meeting, and it had moved with the Prices, to the bungalow they now lived in.

Dawson was now a non-stipendiary minister himself, and was leading the Morning Praise service at St. Nicholas Parish Church – the weekly family service. We attended that also, and it was then that my own lay ministry of preaching began. I can say that it was Dawson's encouragement that empowered me to do this. As is so typical of him, he never hogged the pulpit, but was constantly encouraging members of his congregation to speak. For me it began with a series called "My Faith Journey", where he asked different people from the congregation to share their own faith journey. Then he asked me if I would speak on the Sunday when the Brownies would join us, which they did periodically. At that time there was no Sunday School for the service, and therefore the talks had to be short and appropriate. I did a talk on the Good Samaritan and, as I am quite good at art, I included visual aids. It was so well received that, from then on, Dawson would book me two or three times a year. After a while the service had so many young families, that they started a Sunday School, and the talks after that were addressed to the adults, so visual aids were no longer necessary.

When we moved from Harpenden to Markyate, about the same time that Dawson retired, we began attending a Baptist church, and when the minister discovered I was a speaker at St. Nicholas, she asked me to speak at the Baptist Church. There are lots of little chapels in the area that cannot afford a paid minister, and over the years my speaking engagements have increased to an average of one a month. I still occasionally use visual aids, even when I am speaking to the elderly, because it helps the message to stick! But it all began with Dawson, and I would never have started on this path without his encouragement. He gave me the opportunity to speak that began it all. In my forty-six years as a Christian, I can honestly say that he, above all others, has been the most effective pastor I know in bringing up those under him into their own ministry. All the members of The Group that we are still in touch with, serve the Lord in some sort of ministry, either as clergy or as laity. And when I remember the "nursery" days in The Group that does not surprise me!

But let us to get back to the later days of The Group. The people who immediately spring to mind, as I recall those little meetings in the bungalow, were Rosemary Hill, Hilary Garrett and Lydia Chua. Others members of The Group varied over the years, but those three were there from the time we came back to Harpenden until the meetings finally closed, when Dawson and Norah retired and moved to Fairoak. We are still in touch with all three. Praying with people on a regular basis seems to take the relationship on to a new level, and you can never lose that feeling of "brotherly love" that bonded you as you joined together in prayer.

When Dawson and Norah moved away The Group came to a natural close. And yet it isn't over, is it? Rather like a plant that sheds its seeds and then dies, you know that next season you will still have that bright glow of blooms in your border, and many more than you had originally. So it is with The Group. Its members are scattered across the world now, and they have all had their own sphere of influence. Who can tell what the ultimate harvest will be? What an honour and a privilege to have been a part of it!

COLIN HEARN

My Christian life began when I realised just what sort of mess my life was in. I used to spend most of my time going around with my mates, getting into one lot of trouble after another, although fortunately none of it was really serious. It all started off with a few parties, and drinking in pubs, but in only a short space of time we had got to the point where that wasn't enough. We used to spend Saturday nights going from one party to another, quite often parties where strong drugs were being taken, although we never took hard drugs ourselves. Our drinking habits had changed from cider and beer, to spirits such as gin, vodka and whisky. To us, Sunday was a day when we slept off Saturday night and hoped to be able to face Monday morning.

I had already begun to think about what made everything "tick". I came to the conclusion that there must be some foundation for all the tales of God and other supernatural phenomena, that people talked about. A few friends and myself decided to explore the supernatural, by means of seances and ghost hunts to supposedly haunted places.

It was while all this was happening that I met someone who didn't do the same sort of things as my mates and me, yet seemed to have answers to all the questions that were puzzling me. He told me about Jesus Christ and why He came to Earth, to remove man's sin. At first I used to think that he had his way of thinking and that I had mine, but as time passed I realised that what he was telling me was more than just a theory, that there was something real and solid supporting all that he said. He persuaded me to go to a meeting for young Christians in the town where I live, and in just one evening all my remaining doubts and suspicions were cleared away and I asked the Lord Jesus Christ to come into my life and be my saviour.

Since that night, the Lord Jesus has done many things to help me and to guide me; the more I needed help, the more help He gave me. I have found, however, that as I have progressed in the Christian way of life, I haven't needed so much help, as the situations in which I needed help don't seem to arise any more. Also I get a deep sense of satisfaction out of knowing Jesus, which I cannot compare to anything else that I know.

JEAN HEARN

Jean Hearn joined The Group in the early 1970s. Her two children, Colin and Sally were already attending. Jean was a regular member of The Group until her death in the 80's.

How lucky I am to be blessed with two children! It was through them that I joined a Christian prayer and Bible class. It is through them that I met and made many friends.

Ever since I was a small child I have been going to church, to a small village church with my grandmother, and to Army services held in a large gym, with hundreds of "Call up " boys during the War. I went alone to St. Mary's Church, Bury St. Edmunds, where I was married, my two children - or God's children - were baptised, and I was confirmed. Colin used to ride on my bike to Morning Service.

When I was ill, I always felt better after I had been to church. I have always felt the Lord has been near me, to help and guide me, but I have felt so much closer and nearer since I have joined the Bible class and prayer meetings It is so wonderful to pray and worship God with friends, to feel the Lord is near and with me, never to feel alone or lonely. I thank the Lord for all his blessings and pray for all. I know He hears our prayers. He has been wonderful and helped me so much.

STUART CAVE (Mole)

I was brought up in a good home - upper middle class - and, as a child was forced to go to Sunday School (Congregational Church) in Luton. At the age of twelve or so we moved from Luton to Harpenden, and compulsory church attendance ceased, except for school.

A year or so later, I started going to Crusaders (a sort of Youth Club cum Sunday School) and in four years gave my heart to Jesus three times, but fell away every time. About a year later a friend counselled me about Christianity, and I accepted Jesus yet again, but yet again I fell away. Yet throughout all this, I continued to attend Christian Union at school, until I reached the fifth year, when it faded out. So I lost interest and started living for 'pleasure'. I went to parties, drank and smoked, and my one desire was for girls. Coupled with all this was the fact that I had learned the guitar, and moved in and out of various music groups, both 'pop' and 'folk'.

While singing with one of these groups in 1968, I came into contact with Christ again. I had just left school and was working in a factory, to kill time until my "A" level results came through. A friend went to a Bible study group in Harpenden and some time later suggested that I go along. For a laugh I agreed. At the time I had lost all contact with Christian things, so I thought it would be a good laugh to tell my mates. However, things did not work out the way I expected! These people had something, and all the memories of how I had tried before came back. Maybe Jesus was around after all. One week later, on the Wednesday night, I knelt in prayer and asked Jesus to come into my heart. I did not feel any different, but that did not matter. Every other time I had taken this step I had carried on for somewhere between two and four weeks, so I started as before. This time, however, something different happened.

As I said before, I was singing with a folk group. We were to do a booking in St Albans, so I borrowed my father's Princess 1100, picked up all the members who lived in Harpenden, and went to Luton to pick up one more. On the way back from Luton, travelling at about 50 m.p.h., the car ran out of control, up the bank at a 45 degree angle, and rolled down. Rosemary, in the front passenger seat, and I were flung out as the door burst open! (The doors had burst-proof locks!) I hit the road face down. I was wearing glasses while driving, but these were found intact in the car! It was a case where if we had been wearing safety belts we would not have lived! The car was written off, but all five of us, plus our instruments, survived!

From that day on, Jesus has been with me. He has never left me, and I have stayed with Him. I have strayed from His path, but He has brought me back. No-one can tell me now that Jesus is not alive. I know! He saved my life. Praise His Name!

Looking back, I can see what went wrong when first I asked Christ into my life. I knew all about Him alright, and how I needed Him, but I only knew it in my head. I agreed with it all, but I was not sincere in asking Him in. Finally, however, He proved Himself to me, and I can say in all sincerity, that He lives in my heart.

ANNE GAVITT- Profile

taken from her website on 2009

Anne is a lifelong lover and admirer of animals, and a full-time artist living in Evanston, Illinois, just north of Chicago. She grew up mostly in the Chicago area, part of a family that always included at least one cat. Her love of drawing showed up early, as an occupation that kept her quiet in church, and at last turned into a more serious interest at the end of high school, when she realised she really didn't want to do anything else. Animals have always been a favourite subject of Anne's art. She brings to it her enjoyment of the animals themselves, the light on their fur and in their eyes, their personality and character, their energy.

Anne will work from your photographs, stories, and descriptions to represent in drawing, texture, and colour, what you know and love about your animal friend. She works in graphite pencil and colour pencil. She studied for three years at the American Academy of Art (Chicago), majoring in Illustration, while also taking Watercolour Painting and Lettering and Design. She then worked for a number of years for Moody Bible Institute as an illustrator and production artist, back when cut and paste was done with a knife and rubber cement rather than a mouse click. During and after this time, she took on some freelance work and began to develop her skill with animal portraits. She has illustrated over a dozen children's books and stories, as well as numerous children's magazine stories. When she is not drawing, she may be found playing guitar, singing, experimenting with her own stories and poetry, jogging, or playing softball. She is a member of Reba Place Fellowship, a Christian international community in Evanston.

ANNE GAVITT - 27th April 1970

My parents sent me here, from America, to do two year's sixth form in an English school. I arrived on September 4, and after just a week I was put in contact with Christians in Harpenden. I was invited to a Bible study, and I heard about Jesus in a way that I had never heard before. I could see that these people really loved Him, and I was strongly drawn to want to have this love too.

When still in America, I had gone to church with my family, but I hadn't ever really wanted to go much. I could see that there was some higher kind of life that I was supposed to live, and that I wasn't living it, but I didn't know what to do about it. I guessed that this life should be directed towards, and dedicated to God, but I didn't know how I could do it. Every now and then, I would think about this, and it would sometimes bother me that what waited for me after death was Hell. I guess I had some crazy thought in my head that maybe Hell wasn't going to be all that bad, and so comforted myself with this and forgot about the whole thing. I couldn't be bothered to do "the right thing." I thought it would be a waste of time and energy and life.

So I went on living for myself, doing what I liked. What really hurt me, when I looked back on it recently, is that I took the freedom my parents gave me, the trust and love they gave me, and their faith in my apparent sense, and I used these things wrongly. I did things they taught and trusted me not to do. They knew nothing of it, and if they did question me, I could lie and they would believe me. I didn't want to do this, because I loved my parents, but I had no strength of will over these things.

When I came here and heard about Jesus, I heard about love. Somehow the words went in one ear and out the other, yet I knew that Jesus is love. I'd searched for love, and here it was. Yet still (and I have no idea why) I hesitated.

Then, one evening I was with a few of the Christians, who had talked to me over the previous three weeks. I had said to one of them earlier, that I didn't think I could take the step by myself, so now we all prayed together. I asked Jesus to come into my life. In a moment I knew Jesus was there. It was just one little touch, a feeling. I knew, and I was happy.

Since that moment, a taste of peace, I have learned far more about Jesus than I ever thought there was to know. I gradually began to see more fully how Jesus is the answer to all my questions, doubts and fears, and that He is the perfect loving Friend, that I had been searching for in so many people that had hurt me.

I'd heard also that repentance was a part of following Jesus. Somehow I felt no real conviction until later. I had accepted Jesus because I wanted to be in the love I saw, that my friends were in. This love was the love that Jesus has, and I wanted Jesus. But the real deep conviction came later and when it did I was really burdened by it. I let it weigh on me too much, and let myself go blind and deaf to the Lord. I didn't ask Him for help. I lacked the trust to realise in my heart, what my head knew - that Jesus offered me peace and release, and didn't want me to be this way. What wonderful peace He gave me when I did finally open my heart! I have only recently learned what it is to turn my back on my crucified sin, and really walk away from it with God. It's wonderful!

Another important thing I've learned is that I'll never stop learning or receiving from God. The knowledge that Jesus has forgiven me, and that He loves me, is the first of many wonderful and lasting experiences I know will come. This, I think, is the most important and wonderful thing anyone could ever come to learn. Praise the Lord!

ANNE GAVITT'S STORY - written in 2009

In September of 1969, shortly before my sixteenth birthday, I came to England from Chicago in fulfilment of a plan of my English mother and American dad, to have their children live in the UK and go to school there. My brother had done it from 1966 to 68, and now it was my turn. So I stayed in Harpenden with my godmother, and attended St. Alban's High School. At the end of my first week in the country, a couple of the girls at school took me along to a barbecue at the Congregational Church, where I met Stuart Cave and Martin Hogan. Martin didn't actually introduce himself—he just walked up to the rather bewildered-looking, jet-lagged, slightly homesick young person, handed me an apple and encouraged me to cheer up. Very practical. Equally practical, Stuart gave me a lift home and invited me to a

Bible study. I didn't know what a Bible study was, really, but I knew an opportunity to meet people when I saw one, and agreed to go. A few days later, Stuart gathered me up, drove me to Springfield Crescent, and I walked into Dawson and Norah's house for the first time.

It was a busy, crowded place, lively and friendly. There were something like forty people there, who were divided into two groups for the study. I remember sitting in a big circle, listening to the second chapter of John's Gospel and the story of the cleansing of the Temple. Somehow the conversation got round to something I very much needed to hear. Several people gave testimonies of how they came to the Lord, and how they prayed for guidance or healing. They kept using a phrase, some version of "...and so I asked the Lord to forgive my sins and come into my life." It sounded like a great idea, and I was strongly drawn to this picture of the Christian life.

I had grown up in the Episcopal (Anglican) Church in the USA, and had been given a firm foundation of belief in God and the story of Jesus. But in this Bible study I heard more directly and clearly about the possibility of Jesus being actually in my life, and present to help, strengthen, encourage, change me and grow me up, and that He would never leave me. As the meeting ended with prayer, I prayed the words I had heard: "Jesus, I ask You to please forgive my sins and come into my life." Even though I had no idea what I was asking, God heard me and began to teach me, and kept drawing me in. I came to another Bible study and, over the next week or two, had several conversations with people in The Group about what it was like to live with Jesus.

Although I had prayed that prayer, I was still unsure that anything had "happened". So one evening, when four of us, including Stuart, had been out together — bowling, I believe it was — I asked that they pray with me so I could ask Jesus into my life. We stopped off at one friend's flat and prayed together. As we prayed, I had started to get distracted by some worry about the outcome of all this, when suddenly Jesus felt intensely present and the anxiety just vanished. I was so stunned, that when someone asked me if I had "taken the step" I couldn't for the life of me think what he meant. He asked again and I said, "Yes". A lot of rejoicing followed. The date was October 4th, 1969, and I'd been in England for one month. Quick work, Lord. Thank You!

I have been amazed and grateful to God ever since, for the witness given to me by many individuals in The Group, but even more perhaps, by The Group as a whole. First of all, God was watching over me and guiding me to people who would lead me safely to Jesus and not away from Him, at a time when I would probably have fallen in with just about anyone willing to make friends with me. Once that was taken care of, God used The Group to build a remarkable foundation. On October 4th, 2009, I stood up in my home church here in Evanston and told them some of the things I learned forty years ago, that I cherish as basic truths in my Christian life, beyond the fundamentals of doctrine:

- Jesus loves us and will never leave us.

- Giving our lives to Jesus is the beginning, not the end, of the story.

- Growing in Christ is a lifelong process.

- We can't do it alone.

- We are called into a family and are here to help each other stay close to God.

There is so much more that just that short list, but being in The Harpenden Group is a big part of the way God led me to where I am today. I am a member of a Christian international community called Reba Place Fellowship, a group of about forty people who live near each other, or share living space, and who support one another in various ways, financial and otherwise (that's another whole essay). I have been here for over thirty-two years now, and for almost thirty of those years have sung and played guitar with others in the music ministry of Reba Place Church—something else I began to learn while part of The Group (Thank you, Stuart).

I have worked at various office jobs over the years, gone to art school, and worked as a staff artist at times, or freelanced as a children's illustrator. Right now, I'm nursing along a freelance business of doing drawings of animals, mainly pets.[24] I have been experimenting with writing poetry and stories for a couple of years, and will have a poem published later this fall. Meanwhile, I hold down a part-time office job for a Fellowship-owned property management company, that provides well-maintained low-cost housing for residents in Evanston and the Chicago neighbourhood of Rogers Park, about two miles south. I share a large house in Evanston with

---

24 You can find samples of what Anne's work at www.annegavitt.com, as well as a fairly recent photo.

six other people and three cats (only one of the cats is mine).

I consider The Harpenden Group one of the treasured parts of my history, and am glad to still be in contact with several of you. God's peace go with you!

MAYSIE GREEN

I first met Maysie Green in the autumn of 1972. Lorna and I had started to attend All Saint's Church in Batford. Every year the Church organised a newcomers' evening. Although I had lived in the parish nearly all my life, I usually attended another church, so Lorna and I went along. It was a good evening and we met this very small, rather prim, lady in her mid sixties or early seventies. She had recently moved into Rye Close, not far from where we lived. When she said she was looking for a study group, I invited her to The Group but she did not at first respond. She later telephoned Stewart who was hosting the meeting that evening, and came along.

October 1972

Romans 8 v. 28 We know that in everything God works for good with those who love Him, and are called according to His purpose.

I was brought up in a Christian home, and as a child Jesus was a very real person to me. But throughout the years I have had times of doubt and searching, and have lapsed from grace many times. But I shall always be thankful for that early training in my home.

Four years ago I had a accident and was in hospital for a month, and unable to walk properly for another two months. The Lord did not send this accident, but He used the time of my physical immobility to work on me. At that time I had been a widow for several years, and was on the point of remarrying. It seemed the right step to take, but the Lord had other plans for me, and I was led to see that His plan was better than mine. So I broke the engagement. (Incidentally, I should add that the man I was about to marry is still very good friend, and I have no regrets and I don't think he has either.)

Looking back, I can see that the Lord's plan for me is gradually being fulfilled. He has led me on to a deeper realisation of His love, and a greater understanding of the gift of the Holy Spirit.

I was guided to come to Harpenden almost one year ago, not knowing anyone, except my son and his wife (who have now left Harpenden). After a chain of incidents, I came into the fellowship of this group of Christians, and the joy and fulfilment of that fellowship, guided by the Holy Spirit, is beyond measure.

There is no doubt in my mind that all things work together for good for those who love the Lord.

WILLIAM (Old Bill) POCOCK

One Thursday evening, we had a young, physically handicapped woman present. She had been coming for several weeks. After the meeting she explained that an elderly man had approached her at the day centre and obviously wanted to be friends. At first she misinterpreted his intentions and thought he was proposing to her, and she didn't know what to do. She said that when he learned of her involvement with The Group, he wanted to come. Wanting to keep some of her life private, she had discouraged him, but now didn't know if she had done the right thing. We encouraged her to invite him along and we would discern what was best to do about him.

The next week a taxi drew up and Old Bill arrived. He was a short dumpy man in his middle sixties, freshly widowed, and newly retired from Vauxhall Motors, where he had worked for many years. He was balding and had a grey moustache, and because of severe arthritis, he walked with the aid of two sticks. He was quiet, polite and engaging. We all liked him, and somehow he didn't fit the slightly negative picture we had been given.

Bill really enjoyed the gathering and resolved to come again. Rather than come by taxi it was arranged that one of The Group would collect him and take him home. He became a regular at the meetings, and there was never any sign of a unhealthy attachment to the young woman who first brought him.

After he had been coming for some weeks, we were gathered at Dawson's house for prayer, and Bill was sitting quietly in the corner, obviously in a lot of pain from his arthritis. A some point in the meeting Dawson suggested we should pray for him, and several of us gathered around him to pray, with the laying on of hands. After the meeting I took him home, and arranged to collect him two days later for the Bible study.

The following morning we had a telephone call from Old Bill, to say he had come home on the Tuesday night and gone straight to bed. Usually he was up several times in the night and often awoke early, unable get himself comfortable. That night he slept from 11 pm until 8 am and awoke completely free of pain! He still had arthritis, which deteriorated, causing him to progress from stick to a walking frame. But he never had any more arthritic pain until the day he died, some five years later!

After he had been coming to The Group for some time, he was alone in his flat one day with nothing to do. He distinctly heard a voice say to him "Bill, go and get your Bible and start reading it." Bill wondered what this could mean, because he didn't have a Bible of his own. Then he remembered his wife's Bible was still beside the bed, so he went and got it and sat down in his sitting room. Beginning at the first chapter of Genesis, he began to read it. Now the reader must understand that, although an intelligent man, Bill had never read a book in his life. The limit of his reading, he once told me, was the sports page in the News of the World newspaper. Bill read his Bible twice from cover to cover before he died, and loved every page of it. He especially loved the Psalms, which he read daily.

Bill's life changed dramatically when he found Jesus at The Group. He was lifted up from being a lonely old man with very few friends and an empty life, to being a vibrant Christian man with a huge family who loved him to bits.

During his last year Lorna and I had Robin, who was still a babe in arms. Bill had no children of his own and soon became a grandfather figure for him, and spent a lot of time with us, and enjoyed holding him.

His physical condition deteriorated and Dawson and I went to see him in hospital, just a week before he died.

We read the scriptures to him and prayed with him. Then Dawson prayed for him that the good Lord would take him home. We both knew he would never come home to his flat again. Later that week Bill passed into the loving arms of his Saviour. There weren't many of us at his funeral, which Dawson took at Garston Crematorium. For Lorna and me it was like losing a very close relative. For years we missed his smile and his company. We were so grateful that Old Bill went to spend eternity with his Saviour, and his beloved wife.

OLD BILL (Testimony 1971)

I will start from my young days. I was brought up to go to Sunday School, as my parents were good Christians. My Father was a Deacon and the Sunday School Secretary. As I got older I drifted from the Church and I went my own way, but don't get me wrong, I had a very happy married life. When my dear wife died I became very bored. Then on 29th July 1969 I was introduced to The Group. That evening I gave my heart to our Lord, for it was a night I shall never forget. The Lord worked on me that night and the next morning when I got out of bed, the Lord had taken the pain away from the upper part of my leg and I have not had it since!

I have felt years younger since I have been a Christian. It has made a huge difference to my life.

Now, just before Christmas, I was in my lounge wondering what to do, and I heard a voice saying "Bill, go and get your Bible and read it from the beginning." Now, I have reached Jeremiah Chapter 36. I have never read a book in my life before, but now I know what I was missing. What wonderful reading the Bible is.

Then a few weeks ago, I tore a muscle in my arm and Dawson, and all my friends that were at the meeting prayed for me. Before I went home that evening I could move my arm again!

RUTH FAZAL (née Emmet)

Profile taken from her website 2009

As a worship leader and singer/songwriter, Ruth has travelled extensively across North America, Europe, and Israel, and her deepest desire is to see the body of Christ enter into a truly intimate relationship with Jesus, that goes far beyond corporate worship. Ruth honours and loves the prophetic, and feels an urgency in this hour, for us to be awakened to the purposes of God. Ruth says: "Listening for His voice is the most important thing for us to be doing. I believe that there is a realm that the Lord is wanting to bring us into, in which we will begin to see with a 'Kingdom of God' perspective. I feel sure that it is on God's heart to bring us there, and in that place, for us to come to a greater understanding of who He is, and of who we are in Him. It is time for the Church to be functioning as real citizens of the Kingdom of Heaven. This is what I am giving my heart to! I want to learn how to live that way"

Born in England, Ruth Fazal began her musical studies on the piano and the violin, studying at Dartington College for the Arts, before going on to graduate from the Guildhall School of Music in London. From there, Ruth went on to further studies on the violin in Paris. Since emigrating to Canada, Ruth has performed with all of the major orchestras in the city, as well as being actively involved in many chamber music ensembles. Ruth is currently concertmaster of four different orchestras in the Toronto area, and thoroughly enjoys her musical life in the city. Her most recent classical composition for choirs and symphony orchestra, Oratorio Terezin, has won much critical acclaim both in Canada, Europe, Israel and US. Using the poetry of children from the Holocaust, woven together with the Hebrew scriptures, this work explores the emotions of the heart of God in the midst of human suffering, specifically the suffering of His beloved people Israel during this dark period of history.

News from Canada

The following email was received from Ruth Fazal (née Emmet) on 22nd September 2009 in response to an email from me.

Hi Martin,

How amazing to hear from you, and to know that you are doing this about The Group.

It certainly was an amazing time, and such a foundation of my faith and growth as a young believer.

The thing that has always touched me when I think back is the remarkable cross-section of ages.....from fifteen year olds (myself) to seventy year olds....and there didn't seem to be a dividing line.....everyone was just wanting to know the Lord!

I remember the challenge of faith as we prayed for David's sight to be restored. I remember the Pinkneys' home….. full of people, sitting on the floor. I remember giving my life to the Lord, the first time I came there…. just before Christmas.

I remember the rides in the car to and from meetings, and the wonderful times of worship that we would have, as Bill Kemp would sing and drive! I remember going together to the little Apostolic Church on the green in Welwyn Garden, …. the simplicity of the worship, that taught me from the beginning to not despise simple things (the simple choruses, which I still carry in my heart!)

I remember the prayer meetings at Dawson and Norah's house… I've never been to meetings like that since…. totally unique!

Wow…..what a foundation The Group was to my spiritual life!

PETER HILDEBRAND - *Newsletter February 1974*

Praise the Lord for the changes He has bought about in my life during the past two years.

I was bought up in a very strict Anglican environment and although my father was a good Christian man, (of that I have no doubt), no effort was made to encourage me to communicate with other denominations.

I involved myself in church work without involving myself with God. That, I considered, would come automatically if I went to church regularly, with no effort on my part. Although I realised I was a sinner, my regret over my sins was brought about more from a social conscience than from a love of Jesus Christ.

So it would probably have continued had it not been for a chance conversation one day with Martin Hogan. He started talking to me about something called the "Baptism in the Holy Spirit", which I had never heard of before. However he interested me - what had I been missing? So I went and really read my Bible for the first time. I confess I was simply amazed at what I read - Could all these miracles happen in the modern "souped up" technological age that we live in today? Christianity to my mind applied to the past and to the future; it had very little to do with the present day. Prayers were offered only to ensure you went UP and not DOWN when you gave up the spirit on this Earth. Yet God had created the earth millions of years ago and Jesus Christ was on this Earth under two thousand years ago, a mere drop in the ocean of time compared with the creation of the world. Could it be? I had to know!

So I went to the prayer meeting in Coldharbour Lane, and came away even more amazed! I found that some people really believed the Bible exactly as it was written. This was a lot to swallow.

In an endeavour to find the answer to my questions, I started praying with an earnestness such as never before, together with further Bible reading. Some months elapsed, then it happened!

I generally slept very well, but on the night of the 21st October 1971, I woke up quite suddenly at 3 am with a very clear understanding that I was to go downstairs into the sitting room and PRAY! I confess that I didn't think this was particularly convenient at that hour in the morning and I tried to go back to sleep! But I couldn't sleep, so I tried to reach a compromise by praying flat on my back in bed. This didn't work either, so somewhat aggravated, I got out of bed, mumbled a few words to my wife and went downstairs to do what I had been told to do. After a few moments of prayer I was told that I should attend the prayer meeting at Coldharbour Lane the following evening. Now I was beginning to obey the Lord, and I went back to bed feeling strangely excited, knowing that something would happen that evening but not knowing what that something might be.

The prayer meeting commenced as usual with a Bible reading and then we adopted the most comfortable posture for prayer. After several prayers had been offered I realised that the Lord was instructing me to ask for the Baptism in the Holy Spirit. But how should I ask, and was I ready for this great blessing? Back came the answer (by now I would have been very surprised if I had not received a reply). "Commit yourself to Me entirely. Then ask and it will be given." So I spread out my arms and offered myself to Jesus. How wonderful that was. Praise the Lord! And how easy for anyone who wants to commit themselves to the lord.

As I asked to receive the Baptism, my arms began to tremble, and my body began to shake, yet there was no fear, only a deep indescribable sense of giving myself entirely to the Lord.

By this time the other members of The Group had realised that the Holy Spirit was manifesting Himself and they laid hands on me and prayed. Gradually the trembling subsided, and I was filled with a great joy for what the Lord had done for me. I sang and praised the

Lord all the way home and rushing into my wife declared, "This IS for real. I know Jesus is alive." Up to that point I didn't believe that Jesus' power could show itself on Earth. The pentecostal experience now proved to me that it could, and so turned my beliefs inside out. I knew that anything could happen through Jesus' love for us and by His infinite power.

We were due to go away the following day for a long weekend in the caravan. We had chosen West Mersea in Essex, the Reverend Reg East's old parish. As I strolled along the sands, my life was just one wonderful song of praise. I didn't have to say, "Praise the Lord." although I did quite frequently. I found I was living my praise to the Lord at every moment of the day. In the evening I would go to the sea shore to pray and be with Jesus, just as Simon Peter and Jesus had met on the shore of the Sea of Galilee. What a wonderful weekend it was, but eventually we had to return home.

My prayers continued, for now they had become vitally important, but I had not yet prayed in tongues. That did come one day quite suddenly, when I found I had run out of words with which to praise the Lord and express my love to Him.

About six months ago I became dissatisfied and was beginning to nag the Lord a bit in my prayers. This happened because I was impatient to possess some of the "gifts of the Spirit" about which I had read so much. But I hadn't learned that the Lord does things in His time and that we are bound to go wrong if we try and force the pace.

In the same way that He guided me to ask for the Baptism of the Holy Spirit, I believe He guided me to look back over the past two years of my life, and to recognise the great changes that have taken place. Denominational barriers have broken down, and I have experienced an enormous widening of my Christian commitments, a deeper involvement with brothers and sisters in the Lord and, of course, an awareness of Jesus' love for us. Because of this, everything is being done in the Name of, and for the Glory of God. For these things I Praise the Lord!

I was told the other day, "You can't change the past". I replied "My friend, I wouldn't want to."

Thank you Jesus.

MARGARET BAYLISS (née Strickland)

Margaret sent me these memories on 27th Jan 2010.

I became a Christian through meeting people in The Harpenden Group.

I was fifteen years old, went to church every Sunday with my parents and believed in God. I began going to a youth club at St Nicholas Church in Harpenden. In one of the meetings we had visitors who had come to share their testimonies: Stuart Cave, Chris Williams and his wife Margaret. I think this was my first experience of hearing about God outside of the church liturgy!

Shortly after this our youth club joined the yearly pilgrimage to St Albans Abbey. Groups from all around the Diocese would walk to the Abbey, joining together for a youth service. I remember persuading a friend from school, Linda, to come with me, and we walked from

Harpenden to St Albans, a distance of about 8 miles. Stuart had brought along his guitar and there was much playing of "Oh sinner man, where you gonna run to?" Quite unlike the choruses we sing today! After the service had ended, Stuart asked me, "Do you know Jesus?" I was a bit offended as I was, after all, a regular church-goer, but some realisation at that moment made me say "No." At which point Stuart promptly asked me and Linda to come to a service some friends of his were holding the following week. That was how I found myself in a modern church in Welwyn, at a service being taken by members of The Harpenden Group.

I found out later that David Weston had been going to speak that day but had got a cold and couldn't preach. All I remember was a man springing to his feet, full of intense energy, pacing backwards and forwards and talking to the congregation. I don't remember a word of what he said, but I was gripped with a sense of opportunity and urgency. I felt that this was a moment for me to respond to.

This whole notion of 'becoming' a Christian was completely unknown to me. I went to church and believed in God. I had never before come across any idea of salvation, and certainly had no understanding of a personal relationship with Jesus. All I knew at that moment was that God was giving me a chance at something, and that I had better not miss it!

Another man who had been sitting at the front of the church stood up and asked if anyone would like to come up for prayer. I found myself leaving my seat and the safety of Linda's company, and walking up to the front. I was fifteen years old, extremely self-conscious, and I had a voice shouting in my head; "Sit down! You're making a fool of yourself. Why are you going up? You don't know what you're doing! You don't know what you're going to say!"

I got to the top of the church and looked into the kind face of the man standing there. He took hold of my hands, and I think he asked something like, 'How can I help you?' I was completely confused, but I opened my mouth…and then I heard my own voice saying, "I want to give my life to Jesus." I immediately knew that this was right; this was what I wanted. The voice in my head stopped and my fear left me. Although I didn't know it at the time, this was my introduction to the members of The Harpenden Group. God had, from the beginning of my Christian life, put me in safe hands! The man preaching that day was Bill Kemp, and the man at the front who held my hands was Dawson Price.

I went to The Group in Harpenden for about eight years in all, from 1971 to 1979, from the time I became a Christian at fifteen years old, to the time I left university.

When I look back now, I am filled with such thankfulness to have had The Group as the start and foundation to my Christian life. Most of the best things I know about following Jesus I experienced in our meetings. The Harpenden Group was not an 'instead of church' group. Everyone went to their own churches and were involved with them where they could be. What The Harpenden Group provided was life in the Spirit, worship and a sense of freedom in Christ, which churches in Harpenden largely lacked at that time.

I think I was one of the youngest members of The Group most of the time, although there were other young people. I remember a girl who was a little older than me, and definitely more evangelistic in her school than I was! She would bring her dilemmas to the meetings, and Dawson would listen and very carefully and gently give her any advice which was needed – usually reassurance! Two issues which came up in this way were: should we talk in tongues in front of classmates to show them this spiritual gift, and should long hair be cut short, if it was felt to be a vanity? These make me smile now, but to a teenager trying to be a Christian in the scepticism of school, this was all important stuff!

The Group was a real mixture of ages, from myself in my teens to Old Bill in his sixties.

It was a group of people with whom you were absolutely safe. I was able to share my successes and my troubles and because it was such an inclusive group, I heard about other people's joys and sorrows too, and absorbed an attitude of concern and prayer that stayed alongside the natural self absorption of a teenage girl!

I learnt that I was precious to God and the love of people in The Group reflected this, but I also learnt that it wasn't all about me! An example of this was one evening when Dawson came over to me in the meeting and said that he felt it was time for me to receive the Gift of the Holy Spirit and to speak in tongues. I was terrified! I had been surrounded by the Gifts of the Spirit since first coming to The Group but I was afraid of what this meant – would I be speaking gobbledegook and how would I know that I wasn't? One of the wonderful things about

Dawson and Norah was that they were so calm and practical in their spirituality. This is what God said, so it's true. This is what God promised, so you can have it.

Dawson prayed for me to be filled with the Spirit and I accepted Him. Dawson then encouraged me to try to speak in tongues but I was too self conscious. Seeing this, a little later on, when someone else needed prayer, Dawson suggested I pray for them. So it was whilst I was praying for someone else, that I began to pray in tongues for the first time.

I must have really enjoyed the meetings because I didn't miss very many. We would meet in Dawson and Norah's, Martin and Lorna Hogan's, David and Alma Pinkney's, Old Bill's and Stewart and Carolyn Armour's homes. We would talk, pray, sing and look at the Bible. I remember long times of prayer which would just fly by and much wonderful singing and worship. Stewart Armour, being a choir master and music lover, would complain about the standard of our singing, but we told him that we were sure that God found it beautiful! There was a lot of fun and friendly teasing, as well as the highs and lows of life.

These couples really befriended me and we enjoyed many more times together outside of The Group meetings.

The sense of God's love and community and the work of the Holy Spirit which I found in The Group in those early years of my Christian life have always stayed with me. I cannot imagine that anyone who came to The Group for any length of time would say anything different!

HILARY GARRETT

The Prayer Group 1991-1999

In 1981 I experienced a wonderful life-changing conversion, but ten years later, by 1991, my faith life was seriously "sagging." It was becoming dry, automatic and completely lacking in vitality. It was hard work and joy was noticeably absent! I became aware of how barren my prayer life was – did I even know how to pray?

Around that time, one Sunday, Dawson came to preach at our Anglican Church, St Nicholas, on the subject of prayer – he had my attention! As I listened I realised that here was a man who "knew" about prayer – he made it sound so natural, normal and everyday, not like my strained and tortured efforts. As we left the church, I thanked him for his words, saying how helpful I had found them, as I was struggling in that area. Somewhat to my surprise, he immediately invited me to come to the Friday night prayer group that he had held at his home for many years. I must admit I was a bit surprised, shocked even – I mean – me pray out loud in front of others!

Well, the Friday evening came and I arrived (very nervous) and was immediately put at my ease by Dawson and lovely Norah and the rest of the small but friendly group, about six or seven of us as far as I recall. We started with a short but exciting Bible study led by Dawson on a passage in Isaiah. After this Dawson mentioned one or two possible subjects for prayer and then, with the lights dimmed, he handed the evening over to the Lord for His direction, and we started. It was so peaceful, safe and non-threatening. I even spoke myself. I couldn't believe an hour or so had gone by when Dawson brought it to a close. Then the ever hospitable Norah was there with tea, hot chocolate and scrumptious cakes and biscuits. What an evening! This established a pattern for my Friday nights and I grew in faith as I saw many of the wonderful answers to our prayers. ("Where had I been for the last 10 years?" I asked myself.)

Quite early on, I noticed how frequently The Group mentioned the Holy Spirit and I asked about it. They were encouraging, but allowed me to go at my own pace. Dawson lent me several very helpful books and I became quite desperate to receive the filling of the Holy Spirit. The Group laid hands on me and prayed and I received my first recognisable taste of the Holy Spirit. Further encouragement and teaching led me to a dramatic time of receiving, this time with the Gift of Tongues, for which I had prayed. What an exciting time that was – how it changed my life in so many ways, bringing the Word of God to life as never before! I felt as though my faith was like a boat, which I had been laboriously rowing, when "Someone" whispered that there was an outboard motor, which I only had to start………….

The rest, as they say, is history! I owe Dawson and Norah and The Group, which over the years ebbed and flowed, but never flagged, so much. I met many wonderful people and learned so much from their example.

It is difficult to sum up such a wealth of experiences, but I find that I keep remembering one particular quality of Dawson and Norah. This was their willingness and readiness to accept me exactly as I was - warts, sin and all. They never pushed, judged or preached. I learned (slowly!) by their incredibly patient acceptance and example, of living Christ-like lives in today's busy and, sadly, mostly indifferent world. I am so very grateful to them.

Part 3
The Songs We Sang

From the earliest days of The Group, music was important to us, and over the years we have enjoyed the musical skills of various very talented people, such as Ruth Emmet, Stewart Armour, Chris Williams and Stuart and Sandy Cave.

The era of Stuart and Sandy stands out as a sort of golden age of music for us. This was mainly because they made the music so accessible to even those of us without much talent. Not only could they both play the guitar well, but they would encourage even the learners amongst us to play along with them. I remember a time when I only knew three chords on the guitar, but was able to strum along with Stuart by mirroring the chord shapes as he played. Never once did he complain about my timing or if I missed a chord change, and he was never put off by the mistakes we made. Sandy always gave us a strong vocal lead, which encouraged even those with more timid voices. Not only could they sing and lead the well known choruses, but they were able to introduce us to the many new worship songs that were coming out at that time. They also wrote and sang a lot of their own songs. We were very proud of them in the Lord when they produced their first record, Dawn on Sunday.

In the early days The Group produced The Raise Him Up Song Book Volume 1 and a supplement. The songbook and its supplement had 172 songs, hymns and choruses that we sung regularly, but we also used other publications, including a shortened words-only version of the Redemptionist Hymnal[25], the Hallelujah Chorus Sheet and its Supplement, which contained 157 other songs and choruses, Youth Praise and a number of other sources. At that time many new Christian song books were being published and we used Sounds of Living Waters and other songs of the fisherfolk and Merv and Merla, as well as songs written by Stuart and Sandy, and Ruth Emmet. It was a rich time of writing and many of the songs and choruses of the 70's have become classics today. Here is a list of the songs we sang:

SONGS OF THE GROUP

Raise Him Up Song Book

- Abba Father
- A New Commandment
- Alleluia Alleluia
- All over the World the Spirit is moving
- Alleluia Alleluia give Thanks to the Risen Lord
- Alleluia, Sons of God Arise
- Amazing Grace
- And Can it Be
- All Hail the Power of Jesu's Name
- Ask, and it Shall be Given You
- At the Name of Jesus, Every Knee Shall Bow
- Breath on me Breath of God
- By Your Stripes, Lord, I'm Healed,
- Blessed is the Man

---

25 *The Redemption Hymnal* is a red-covered hymnbook containing 800 evangelical hymns, first published by the Elim Publishing House in London, in 1951. The hymnal is strongly associated with the emergence of the Pentecostal movement in the United Kingdom

- Bless the Lord O my Soul
- Bind us Together Lord
- Burdens are Lifted at Calvary
- Break Forth into Joy, O my Soul
- Break Thou the Bread of Life
- Beneath the Cross of Jesus
- Blessed Assurance, Jesus is Mine
- By Blue Galilee
- Christ is Alive Today
- Come Bless the Lord, all ye Servants of the Lord
- Clap your Hands, all you People
- Crown Him with Many Crowns
- Can it be True
- Clean Hands or Dirty Hands
- Come Walk with me Round the Walls of the City
- Don't try to Tell me that God is Dead
- Dear Lord I Appreciate You
- Dear Lord and Father of Mankind
- Fill my Cup Lord
- For me to Live is Christ
- Friend of Mine, Friend Divine
- Follow, Follow, I will Follow Jesus
- He is my Everything
- For a Day in thy Courts is Better than a Thousand
- For Thou art Great and Doest Wondrous Things
- Father I Adore You
- Gone, Gone, Gone, Gone, Yes my Sins are Gone
- Give me Joy in my heart
- God can do Anything, Anytime, Anywhere
- Great is Thy Faithfulness
- Guide me O Thou Great Jehovah

- Glory to Thee my God this Night
- Glorious Things of Thee are Spoken
- God Forgave my Sins in Jesus Name
- God has Called You
- Great is the Lord, and Greatly to be Praised
- Go Forth and Tell
- His Name is Wonderful
- His Name is Jesus, Jesus
- He Lives! He Lives!
- Higher than the Hills
- He's the Saviour of my Soul
- How Great is our God
- How Great Thou Art
- He is Lord, He is Lord
- His Name is like an Ointment Poured Forth
- He Shall Flow like a River
- He Welcomes me to His Banqueting Table
- Hallelujah, for the Lord our God, the Almighty Reigns
- Holy, Holy
- He Touched me, He Touched me
- Ho Everyone that is Thirsty in Spirit
- Here Comes Jesus, See Him Walking on the Water
- O Lord Most High, Most Holy God and Saviour
- In the Name of Jesus.. We have the Victory
- I am Covered Over with the Robe of Righteousness
- I'm Rejoicing Night and Day
- I've Found the Answer, I've Learned to Pray
- I Danced in the Morning
- I will Sing the Wondrous Story
- I Heard the Voice of Jesus Say
- I Heard a Thousand Trumpets

- I love the Lord, and He loves Me
- I stand Amazed in the Presence
- I've taken my Harp down from the Willow tree
- I am the Bread of Life
- I'm Living in Hallelujah Land
- All to Jesus I Surrender
- If you want Joy, Real Joy
- I get so thrilled with Jesus
- If that Same Spirit that Raised Christ from the Dead
- It is Joy Unspeakable and Full of Glory
- I was Glad, very Glad When They Said to me
- Just a Closer Walk with Thee
- In my Heart there Rings a Melody
- I love, I love that Man of Galilee
- I want to Walk as a Child of the Light
- It's me, it's me, it's me, O Lord
- I'll Sing of His Goodness, I'll Sing of his Grace
- I want to Live for Jesus Everyday
- Jesus took my Burdens and He Rolled them in the Sea
- Jesus is Alive, Jesus is Alive
- Jesus is Knocking, Patiently Waiting
- Jesus I love you, Jesus I Love you
- Just as I am, Without one Plea
- Lifted, I've been Lifted
- Jesus is Lord, Creation's Voice Proclaims It
- Jesus Jesus, Let me tell You how I Feel
- Jesus how Lovely You are
- Jesus' Love is Very Wonderful
- Joy is the Flag Flown High
- Let all that is Within me Cry Holy
- Let my Spirit Work among You

- Lord of all Hopefulness
- Let's Talk about Jesus
- Living He loved me
- Loved with Everlasting Love
- Lovely Name, Jesus
- Let us Break Bread Together
- My Song is Love Unknown
- Man of Sorrows, What a Name
- Praise Him, Praise Him
- Morning has Broken
- My God can do Anything
- Now Thank we all our God
- O for a Thousand Tongues to Sing
- Only Believe, Only Believe
- O Lord, all the World Belongs to You
- Our Father, who art in Heaven
- O Happy day that Fixed my Choice
- Oh, how I Love Jesus
- Oh the Blood of Jesus
- Peace is Flowing like a River
- Pass me not O Gentle Saviour
- Praise God from Whom all Blessings Flow
- Reach out and Touch the Lord
- Rolled Away, Rolled Away
- Seek ye First the Kingdom of God
- Silver and Gold have I None
- Something in my Heart like a Stream Running Free
- Son of God, Son of God
- Spirit of the Living God
- Stand up, Stand up for Jesus
- Surely Goodness and Mercy Shall Follow Me

- Take my Hand and Follow Me
- Tell out my Soul
- Thou art Worthy, Thou Art Worthy
- The King of Love my Shepherd is
- Turn your Eyes upon Jesus
- This is my Commandment that you Love one Another
- The Joy of the Lord is my Strength
- The Lion of Judah
- The Lord's my Shepherd
- There's Going to be a Meeting in the Air
- Thank you Lord for Saving my Soul
- Thine be the Glory, Risen Conquering Son
- This is the Day, This is the Day
- To be Like Jesus, to be Like Jesus
- The Law of the Lord is Perfect
- To God be the Glory, Great Things He has Done
- The Lord is my Shepherd I'll walk with him Always
- The King and I Walk Down Life's Road Together
- Therefore the Redeemed of the Lord Shall Return
- Thine Forever, God of Love
- Thy Loving Kindness, is Better than Life
- Trust and Obey
- Who can Cheer the Heart like Jesus
- We see the Lord, We See the Lord
- We are One in the Spirit
- Wonderful, Marvellous is Jesus to Me
- What a Friend we Have in Jesus
- Wide Wide as the Ocean
- When I Survey the Wondrous Cross
- Yesterday, Today, Forever

These may seem very dated now, but at the time most of the choruses were the latest! Christian music and song writing have come on a long way in the last 40 years. Many of the choruses we sang are unheard of now, but we really sang them with gusto and many times would find ourselves in heavenly places as we sang. None of the singing was planned beforehand. People would ask for the song they wanted, or sometimes the Spirit would move us to sing, and the musicians joined in. Worship in song was incredibly infectious and meetings of any sort didn't feel right without a good time of worship in song beforehand. I often look back and wish I could sing again as we used to sing, but alas my voice croaks now!

Finally

In this book I have tried to help you enter into the spirit of those wonderful times and to read first-hand testimonies and memories. I hope I have shown how God has led us by His Holy Spirit each step of the way. In a way it is like Acts 28, the continuing story. But the Acts of the Apostles didn't end in Chapter 28, or even in the 1970's; it continues in every generation. Many of the testimonies are given by teenagers, and you might easily dismiss them as 'kids who hadn't lived yet'. But it is true that in every Christian movement and revival the key people are young and green! As I have contacted so many of The Group thirty to forty years on, I have been amazed and thrilled how God has held them, used them and furthered the work of His Kingdom through them.

But, as I say, the story doesn't end here. The next generation must write their story too. In the meantime, the subject of another book might well be the testimonies of The Harpenden Group from the time they left The Group to the present day. I would say that would be a wonderful story. Well done for getting this far and may the Lord Jesus bless you in all you do for Him.